Sex and Sexuality in Georgian Britain

Dedicated to Emma and Jo: no daughters should have to suffer the embarrassment of a father who writes about sex and sexuality!

Sex and Sexuality in Georgian Britain

Mike Rendell

First published in Great Britain in 2020 by
Pen & Sword History
An imprint of
Pen & Sword Books Ltd
Yorkshire – Philadelphia

Copyright © Mike Rendell 2020

ISBN 978 1 52675 562 9

The right of Mike Rendell to be identified as Author of this work has been asserted by him in accordance with the Copyright, Designs and Patents Act 1988.

A CIP catalogue record for this book is
available from the British Library.

All rights reserved. No part of this book may be reproduced or transmitted in any form or by any means, electronic or mechanical including photocopying, recording or by any information storage and retrieval system, without permission from the Publisher in writing.

Typeset by Mac Style
Printed and bound in the UK by TJ Books Limited,
Padstow, Cornwall.

Pen & Sword Books Limited incorporates the imprints of Atlas, Archaeology, Aviation, Discovery, Family History, Fiction, History, Maritime, Military, Military Classics, Politics, Select, Transport, True Crime, Air World, Frontline Publishing, Leo Cooper, Remember When, Seaforth Publishing, The Praetorian Press, Wharncliffe Local History, Wharncliffe Transport, Wharncliffe True Crime and White Owl.

For a complete list of Pen & Sword titles please contact

PEN & SWORD BOOKS LIMITED
47 Church Street, Barnsley, South Yorkshire, S70 2AS, England
E-mail: enquiries@pen-and-sword.co.uk
Website: www.pen-and-sword.co.uk

Or

PEN AND SWORD BOOKS
1950 Lawrence Rd, Havertown, PA 19083, USA
E-mail: Uspen-and-sword@casematepublishers.com
Website: www.penandswordbooks.com

Contents

Preface		vi
Chapter 1	Matters Medical	1
Chapter 2	London: As Others Saw Us	10
Chapter 3	How Royalty and the Rich Behaved	23
Chapter 4	Courtesans, Celebrity Whores and Fashionistas	35
Chapter 5	Of Virginity and Masturbation, of Dildos and Sex Aids	52
Chapter 6	Aphrodisiacs, Libido and Fertility	62
Chapter 7	Ways of Avoiding Pregnancy: Including Contraception and Abortion	71
Chapter 8	Sexually Transmitted Diseases and their Treatment	81
Chapter 9	Rape	94
Chapter 10	Bigamy, Bestiality and Brothel-keeping	107
Chapter 11	Where it All Happened: Brothels, Bagnios and Jelly Houses	116
Chapter 12	Sodomites	126
Chapter 13	Sapphites, Flagellation and Cross-dressers	140
Chapter 14	Sex and Sexuality in Eighteenth-century Literature and Art	153
Conclusion		165
Appendix 1		169
Appendix 2		177
Bibliography		183
Index		189

Preface

This book is intended to look at sex and sexuality in the period between 1714, when the first George came to the throne, and 1837, the accession of Queen Victoria. But of course, personal things such as sexual proclivities do not change merely because a different monarch sits on the throne, and it is sometimes helpful to look back at what happened in the 1600s to see how this shaped subsequent events. Besides, history is not so much a series of equally-weighted pendulum swings as a few tumultuous events followed by a series of aftershocks. That was certainly true of the previous century, which saw the execution of Charles I, the Commonwealth of Oliver Cromwell and the emergence of the Puritans, followed by the Restoration of the Monarchy. Things did not suddenly settle down after that and society felt the repercussions

Fashionable contrasts. (You know what they say about men with big feet....)

as conflicting pressures emerged: pressures from the church, pressures from the state, and economic pressures.

Someone living in 1700 may well have been alive when poor Susan Bounty, a married woman from Bideford in Devon, was led to the gallows in 1654, the last person to be hanged for the 'awful crime' of adultery, after she had given birth to a child not fathered by her husband. That person may also have read the poems of the aristocrat John Wilmot, 2nd Earl of Rochester, who fearlessly mocked Charles II, ridiculed the court, committed blasphemy, and was dead, quite possibly from venereal disease, by the age of thirty-three. The observer from his or her viewpoint in 1700 would also have heard of the twenty-year-old Thomas Aikenhead, hanged for the offence of blasphemy in 1695. The point here is that the role of the State in determining what the individual could do, say or think was still being debated, and the debate was to dominate the Georgian era.

During the eighteenth century there were conflicting moves: some pulled in the direction of greater personal freedom of choice, while others sought to re-establish State control through censorship, using laws against sedition, libel and blasphemy. Theatres were banned from putting on plays unless they had been approved by the Lord Chamberlain. Plays critical of the government were unlikely to get their place under the spotlight of the stage and therefore works such as John Gay's *Polly*, the follow-up to *The Beggar's Opera*, were never performed.

Seditious libel had long been a concept under Common Law, and was used by the courts to punish anything deemed to be tending towards insurrection against the established order. Seditious libel and blasphemous libel were considered to be interchangeable descriptions of an offence which could be committed against the king, his government or the established church. It was a charge used against the poet Leigh Hunt as late as 1812 in retaliation for his rude comments about the Prince of Wales, calling him fat, oily and like a whale. And yet the existence of a law against seditious libel did not prevent Gillray, the doyen of satirists, from portraying the king and his family in the most disparaging and critical manner. Showing an image of the queen as a hideous old hag with bare breasts and with her hand covering the groin of the (naked) William Pitt, *'Sin Death and the Devil'* implied that the wife of the monarch was having a sexual relationship with the prime minister. Yet no charges were brought against Gillray for this most scurrilous of prints.

It is easy to forget how nervous the House of Hanover must have felt throughout the eighteenth century. Not only did it have the example of regicide as a reminder from the previous century, but it also had to face the very real threat of a Jacobite Revolution, not just in 1715 and 1745, but with the general undercurrent of feeling against the nation's rulers. How much more those royal nerves must have suffered when, towards the end of the century, the French Revolution showed the fragility with which the royal head rested upon royal shoulders.

Throughout the century there were moves to reduce the powers of both the monarchy and its government and allow greater individual freedom. Conversely, it led to men like the radical John Wilkes, editor of the influential publication *North Briton,* and a fervent supporter of the rights of the individual. He championed the reporting of parliamentary proceedings, and in 1776 introduced the first ever bill for parliamentary reform.

Nowhere was the debate about freedom more apparent than in the battle between the commercial interests of the landed gentry (and in particular, plantation owners) and the rights of the oppressed – the slaves – whose rights were promoted by influential Quakers. However, it wasn't just a fight about the rights and wrongs of slavery; it was also about the much wider question of what freedom meant, what freedom of expression amounted to, what freedom to live out your life according to your personal beliefs and standards really involved. It was never a gradual path, and along the way there were attempts to impose greater controls; the growth of groups such as the Society for the Reformation of Manners being one example, the trial of John Wilkes for seditious libel another. Later, in 1792 and 1793, sedition trials were brought against a group of individuals calling for parliamentary reform, and two years later thirty men were charged with high treason in an attempt by the government to destroy the British radical movement. When the trials collapsed the government was forced to pass two 'gagging acts' (the Seditious Meetings Act and the Treasonable Practices Act, both in 1795). But while these great ideals of freedom were being passionately debated, the man-in-the-street just got on with living his life. Perhaps John Wilkes got it right when he sagely observed in his *Essay on Woman* (a bawdy parody of Pope's *Essay on Man*), 'life can little more supply/Than just a few good fucks and then we die.'

Freedom always existed on two levels: as a noble concept fought over and proclaimed by politicians and journalists; and as a sort of mantra for bloody-minded individuals ('This Englishman's home is his castle: it's my life and I will damned well live it how I want'). As long as John Bull was free to fornicate when he wanted, with whoever he wanted, then he probably was not too worried about who got the vote.

While the eighteenth century saw a much more open discussion about sexual matters it did not mean that the floodgates were opened evenly. Men could still be forced to pay massive damages for what was known as criminal conversation (adultery, in other words). Witness the case of the Duke of Cumberland, brother to His Majesty King George III. Caught *in flagrante* with the wife of Lord Grosvenor in 1769, he was ordered to pay damages to His Lordship amounting to what would nowadays be around one million pounds.

A relaxation in legal penalties did not stop moral crusaders from trying to tug the moral tide back towards puritanism, and it would be a mistake to see the eighteenth century as a smooth progression towards sexual freedom of choice. There were remarkable excesses – the behaviour of the Prince of Wales, who deserves his epithet as the Randy Regent, springs to mind – but there were also attempts by the Church and the State to re-impose rules relating to human behaviour.

Taken as a whole, the eighteenth century saw great changes in the way sexual behaviour was regarded. But then came Mary Wollstonecraft: a woman who lived openly with her lover, who had a child by him and who had tried to commit suicide not once but twice, and who stuck the proverbial two fingers up at anyone who disapproved of her lifestyle. In so doing she probably set back her cause by a hundred years. Nowadays she may be regarded as a proto-feminist, at the vanguard of the movement towards equality, but two centuries ago the public were horrified at her lifestyle and people turned their backs on her ideas. It just went to show that the ebb and flow of the moral tide was never smooth, and there were always exceptions that proved the rule.

More than anything else the century saw a dichotomy: a split between what was acceptable for the rich and what was acceptable for the poor; a split between the aristocracy and the general public; and above all, a schism between what was acceptable in London and what was acceptable in the country. It was an exciting century: a period of change, adventure, discovery, openness and glamour. It was an era when sex workers could strut their stuff in outfits which would have done justice to a duchess, where hookers attended masquerade balls dressed as nuns and hoped to get off with a prince dressed as a farmhand. It was a century when stories of adultery ensured that divorce trial reports were sensational reading for a prurient public. It was an era when you could visit the Summer Exhibition of the Royal Academy and see the portrait of a leading royal hanging next to the most infamous courtesan. It was also an era when venereal disease wrought havoc with the bodies of tens of thousands of men, women and children. Celebrity status was bestowed, then as now, upon the most unworthy of recipients. And if we want to examine the sexual hypocrisy of our present era we can do no better than look at the hypocrisy of the eighteenth century.

Sin, Death and the Devil – suggesting that the (naked) Prime Minister was having an affair with the Queen.

Chapter 1

Matters Medical

Ah, the eighteenth century: the Age of Reason, a.k.a. the Age of Enlightenment! Such terms are bandied about as if the new century was marked by a light being turned on, illuminating the dark corners of ignorance in a single movement. It was not, of course, anything like that. In many ways the century remained an era of uninformed superstition, no more so than in the area of understanding sexual desire, and the mechanics of the human body and reproduction.

Take the extraordinary case of Godalming woman Mary Toft. In 1726 she became pregnant. In the words of *Mist's Weekly Journal*, 'the woman hath made Oath, that two Months ago, being working in a Field with other Women, they put up a Rabbit, who running from them, they

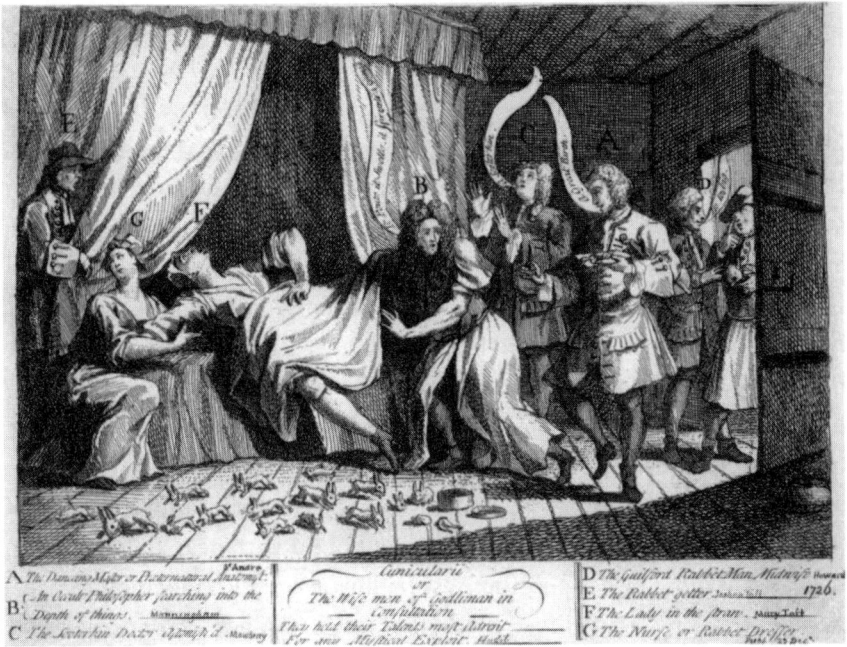

William Hogarth's take on the story of Mary Toft, giving birth to numerous rabbits ...

pursued it, but to no Purpose: This created in her such a Longing to it, that she (being with Child) was taken ill and miscarried, and from that Time she hath not been able to avoid thinking of Rabbits.'

Mary went on to claim that following the miscarriage she gave birth to various rabbits and other animal parts. Some of these pieces of flesh were sent to John Howard, a man-midwife of thirty years' experience who lived in nearby Guildford. He may have been dubious, but nevertheless he visited Mary, whereupon she 'gave birth' to 'three legs of a Cat of a Tabby Colour, and one leg of a Rabbet.'

News of the extraordinary 'birth' reached London and was quickly reported in the national press, and in early November a man called Henry Davenant went to see for himself what was happening. The gullible Davenant, a member of the court of King George I, appeared to accept everything at face value, and wrote a number of letters seeking to share his remarkable discovery with various members of the medical profession. The case came to the attention of the surgeon to the Royal Household, a Swiss gentleman by the name of Nathaniel St André. In fairness, St André probably owed his position at court solely to the fact that he spoke German, a prerequisite in the court of the first Hanoverian king.

Mary was by now enjoying her moment of fame, her place in the spotlight, and happily produced a number of lagomorph (i.e. bunny parts) from her nether regions. Other doctors were called on for their opinions. Some, such as John Maubray, were keen to endorse the story because it supported the belief in maternal impression; the idea that conception and pregnancy could be affected by the dreams of the pregnant mother. In *The Female Physician* Maubray had warned pregnant women that overfamiliarity with household pets could cause their children to resemble those pets. He wrote: 'Suppose [a woman] conceives in her mind some deformed Spirit or Animal, with Horns, Snout, Wings, Cloven Feet etc (as has sometimes happened): What should hinder this woman to produce a birth with these monstrous marks?' Indeed, he maintained that it was 'perfectly common for women to mark her child with pears, plums, milk, wine or anything else, upon the least trifling accident happening to her.'

Despite being a qualified physician and a teacher of midwifery, he maintained that women could give birth to tiny creatures called sooterkins, about the size of a mouse. This idea had been prevalent in Holland, where women were allegedly inclined to sit on top of their cooking stoves, and this 'incubation' was believed to cause sooterkins to develop.

On 3 December 1726 St André published a forty-page pamphlet detailing the extraordinary story. His timing was poor. The following day Mary was forced to make an admission that she had fabricated the entire story, and that she had simply inserted animal parts into her vagina as a short-cut to fame, and fortune.

The entire hoax caused the medical profession to be held up to ridicule. But the underlying idea of maternal impression remained powerful, with echoes in folkloric stories that being startled by a hare could cause a child to be born with a hare-lip and that eating too many lobsters could cause port-wine stain birthmarks. A century later there were still so-called experts who believed that the deformities exhibited by Joseph Merrick (the 'Elephant Man') were the result of his mother being startled by a pachyderm.

But if the medical profession emerged from the Mary Toft case in a poor light, it was no more than it deserved. For much of the century, medicine followed the Galen theory of the four humours. Galen, the Anglicized name of Claudius Galenus, was a Greek physician, surgeon and philosopher in the Roman Empire. Since the time of Aristotle and Socrates the idea of the body being made up of a combination of hot, dry, cold and wet components (fire, air, earth and water) led physicians to the idea of treatment by opposites. Balance was necessary, even if it meant using enemas, laxatives, blood-letting and violent purging to try to establish equilibrium in a sick patient. The theory held that the four humours existed as liquids within the body and were identified as blood, phlegm, black bile and yellow bile. Youth was hot and moist, age was dry and cold, and men as a sex were hotter and drier than women. A woman's menstrual cycle was simply an example of imbalance: a woman's body was softer and more like a sponge than a man's and therefore needed to be emptied of excess blood on a regular basis. If it was not emptied during a monthly period, then a nose bleed – or vomiting blood – was seen as a perfectly normal alternative.

There was very little understanding about ovulation, and no comprehension that the menstrual cycle involved the shedding of the lining of the womb. It was just thought that it represented the discharge of an excessive build-up of liquid from all over the body. It follows from this that the medical knowledge of conception and contraception were rudimentary to say the least. It is more likely that a woman would know rather more about the workings of her body than the vast majority of the medical profession. William Harvey may have published his book on the function of the heart and the circulation of blood in 1626, but doctors a century later still believed that if a woman did not have a regular period she would have to be bled from a vein in her arm. Furthermore, even the renowned anatomist and physician William Hunter maintained that the uterus was capable of moving around thereby causing delirium, melancholy and frenzied paroxysms.

The reproduction argument, with the battle of the sexes as to who was most important for reproduction, had kicked off in 1678 when the Royal Society published its *Philosophical Transactions* containing a paper by an obscure Dutch shopkeeper called Antony van Leeuwenhoek. Devoid of scientific training or academic qualifications, Leeuwenhoek had developed lenses for the compound microscope and had spent his time looking at the usual small objects – the stinging mechanism of the bee, microscopic pond-life, bacteria in tooth plaque and so on – until he hit on the idea of examining his own ejaculant. He was the first to observe the tadpole-like sperm wriggling their way through the seminal fluid, but left it to others to try to work out the significance of what he had observed. He was apparently somewhat abashed at submitting his findings to the Royal Society in London, writing: 'If your Lordship should consider that these observations may disgust or scandalise the learned, I earnestly beg your Lordship to regard them as private and to publish or destroy them as your Lordship sees fit.' Other scientists then embroidered his findings, drawing pictures imagining what they might be looking at under their own microscopes, including one by Nicolaas Hartsoeker drawn in 1695 and shown at the end of this chapter.

Throughout the eighteenth century scientists had been peering through their microscopes examining human sperm, and had come up with two separate hypotheses as to what they were looking at. Those who saw the male role in reproduction as all-important believed that each sperm consisted of a fully-formed but tiny homunculus. These were planted in the woman, who simply acted as an incubator. On the other side were the ovists, who maintained that there must be some sort of egg, produced by the woman, and containing a pre-formed embryo which grew inside her without male intervention. Some even argued that coition was not needed for reproduction.

The argument between the 'pre-formists' (whether fully formed in the male sperm or in the woman's egg) slowly gave way in the middle of the eighteenth century to the 'epigenesists' who argued that both males and females contributed to form a new organism. In 1759 it was discovered that chicks develop organs incrementally. The problem for the epigenerists was that no one was sure 'who contributed what' to the process and it was not until 1827 that Karl Ernst von Baer discovered the human ovum.

It was small wonder that in this vacuum of knowledge the medical profession, all of them male, made something of a hash of understanding menstruation. A young woman with irregular periods was thought to be suffering from the green sickness, a sure sign that she should be married off so that regular sex could help prevent a build-up of unhealthy humours. Nowadays we may identify the condition as hypochromic anaemia, but as late as 1803 the *Edinburgh Practice of Physic, Surgery and Midwifery* explained that 'love and other passions of the mind' cause *chlorosis amatoria*, otherwise known as the 'green sickness'. This was exhibited by insufficient menstrual blood being produced by women. Francis Grose, in his *Dictionary of the Vulgar Tongue*, published in 1811, defined 'green sickness' as 'the disease of maids occasioned by celibacy.' Love-sickness was an imbalance, exacerbated and inflamed by the reading of amorous novels. Sex was the obvious cure. And so we had a 1705 ballad called *Enfield Common* in which a 'fair maiden' suffering from green sickness is enthusiastically cured by a 'lusty gallant' who manages to 'ease her, and fully please her'. In his words:

> Then in a minute I left my Ginnet*,
> and went aside with her into a Thicket,
> Then with her leave there, a dose I gave her,
> she straight confess'd her Sickness I did nick it.

---

* (A ginnet was a name for a small horse).

To quote from John Maubray, here was a disease peculiar to mature virgins, and a disagreeable affliction of the body: 'The Virgin disease is a change in the natural colour of the face into a pallid greenish tincture with a dejection of strength'. It caused heaviness of the heart, fever, pains, melancholy and palpitations, to say nothing of 'oedemerous tumours of the feet'. The cure? Good diet, abstinence from morning lie-ins (in case the vapours ascended to the brain) and regular purging and blood-letting. A girl needed to be rubbed down every morning with a warm flannel, especially effective in the spring and summer, but less so in the winter or when it was cold outside. The final piece of the jigsaw was to marry her off, thereby 'preventing all the future ill consequences of this growing Malady'. For 'marriage' read 'regular sex': a maiden could not be expected to obtain sexual gratification except within marriage.

It was another example of male double standards: a world in which an adulterous man was known as a 'gallant', or as a person who 'intrigued'. They were rakes or roués, whereas a woman behaving in a similar manner could be judged as being a whore, a slut or a loose woman. (Whoever heard of a 'loose man'?).

Mind you, Maubray also believed that if a virgin had an excess of blood in her body this would be turned into breast milk by the 'peculiar faculty of the breast'. It differed from lactation in young mothers because the milk was thinner, more watery. But there again, a virgin could always be detected because her urine was crystal clear.

This was a time when hysteria (from the Greek word *hysterika*, meaning uterus) was still believed to be a female complaint linked to an imbalance of the humours. A retention of fluids in the uterus was believed to cause the uterus to wander around the female body causing irritability and putting pressure on other internal organs. In the eighteenth century this could result in the poor woman being incarcerated in a mental hospital for years on end. Excessive emotion was definitely not to be permitted, and after all, no man would be safe with a woman roaming around in desperate need of sex! This idea of a uterus wandering around the female body careering into other organs and upsetting the balances of things was not finally disproved until 1761, with the publication of *The Seats and Causes of Diseases* by the eminent Italian physician G.B. Morgagni.

Hysteria could affect virgins and widows alike. In Maubray's book both the man and the woman produced a seed, and if the one inside the woman was not used it could cause problems: 'Of the Hysterick Passion: I take it that the too long retained seed to occasion the more dangerous and severe symptoms to the woman.'

These symptoms could 'cause malignant vapours to rise' in the woman's body, with different symptoms according to where the build-up occurred: in the heart (palpitations and anxiety), or the head (senseless stupidity, linked to trembling and convulsive fits) and so on. Nervousness and problems with the nervous system ('neurologie') were suspected of causing many female ailments, while others lay the blame firmly on 'the Stomach and Guts, whereof the grumbling of the one and the Heaviness and Unease of the other' could led to paroxysms. So said John Purcell, a physician working in London in the first two decades of the eighteenth century. To him, it was quite clear: vapours from the stomach rose up to the head and caused 'Hysterick Fits', a disease which could 'transform itself into the shape and representation of almost all distempers.'

Things hadn't really progressed far since Pliny the Elder identified the magical powers possessed by menstrual blood: it could control the weather by stopping hail storms; it could kill crops and bees; make sharp blades blunt and dull the reflection in mirrors; and it could make wine taste sour. Seventeen hundred years later and men still thought that a woman's menstrual cycle prevented her from getting butter to churn properly, and meant that hams would not cure when immersed in salt.

It needs to be borne in mind that the eighteenth century was a time when men believed that they knew what was best: they ruled the Church, and hence controlled religious instruction; they alone could be medical practitioners; they alone could carry out anatomy dissections; and they alone could pontificate on matters which nowadays would be regarded as female issues. Take giving birth: the aforementioned John Maubray in his book *The Female Physician* (or, to give it its full title, *The Female Physician containing all the Diseases incident to that Sex in Virgins, Wives and Widows*) was able to write: 'men [...] being better versed in Anatomy, better acquainted with Physical Helps, and commonly endued with greater presence of Mind, have been always found readier or discreeter, to devise something new, and to give quicker Relief in Cases of difficult or preternatural births, than common midwives generally understand.'

For Maubray there was no problem in defining when human life was formed; it was fifty days after the formation of the embryo. At that stage the human soul was formed ('the animation of the foetus'). It followed from this that terminating the pregnancy during those first fifty days was not abortion, but a form of contraception. This found an echo in later ideas that it was only a crime to terminate after the first signs of quickening; roughly between sixteen and eighteen weeks, when the unborn child could be felt kicking.

The supposed male superiority meant that men were better able to diagnose the problems caused by strong sexual urges. In men it was of course entirely natural. They had been endowed with a penis, and the urge to use it, and therefore it was entirely proper that if they could not find sexual gratification within marriage, they should look for a release in some other way: through having a mistress, or using prostitutes. Women on the other hand needed to be protected from their carnal desires. As will be seen in later chapters, medical ignorance extended to an inaccurate understanding of contraception and a total failure to differentiate between syphilis and gonorrhoea. It all adds to the suspicion that whereas we may like to refer to the eighteenth century as the Age of Reason, it can more accurately be described as the Age of Confusion.

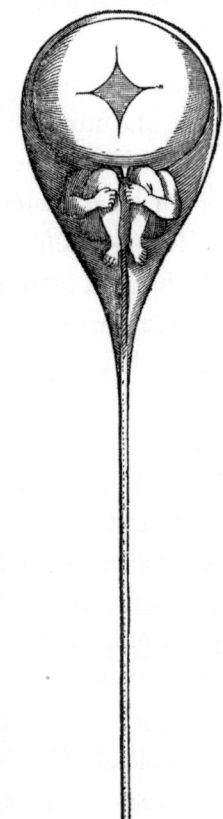

Superstition still reared its ugly head whenever it was given the chance. And so it was that when two earthquakes were felt in London on eighth February and eighth March 1750, the Bishop of London was able to clamber into his pulpit and explain to the congregation that the 'quakes were caused by Divine displeasure ... at pornography. John Cleland's *Memoirs of a Woman of Pleasure* (otherwise known as *Fanny Hill*) had just been published. And in case we think that such ideas are outdated it is worth remembering that when

The human sperm under a microscope, imagined.

the Indonesian province of Banda Aceh was devastated by an earthquake and giant tsunami on Boxing Day 2004, religious leaders in that country were quick to attribute the cause to divine anger at human immorality. Remember, too, that we still define earthquakes as 'Acts of God' in our insurance policies.

Chapter 2

London: As Others Saw Us

One way of gaining an eighteenth-century view of our moral compass is to look at how our European neighbours saw us. César-François de Saussure, who had been born in 1705 and died in 1783, was a Swiss travel writer who arrived in London in May 1725 and stayed until October 1729. He then travelled to Turkey and Switzerland before returning to London between 1738 and 1740. His assessment? 'An immeasurable number of Englishmen are still more corrupt in their morals than in their religion. Debauch runs riot with an unblushing countenance.'

The contest between the spirit and the flesh, showing a young man pulled in opposite directions by a prostitute and a religious lady.

Another visitor was Frenchman Pierre-Jean Grosley, a French travel writer born in 1718. He was outraged at the sight of hordes of prostitutes parading their wares for sale in public places: 'whole rows of these unhappy women accost passengers in broad daylight'. To his amazement these street walkers enjoyed notoriety, if not fame: 'the list of those who are in any way eminent is publicly cried about the streets. This list, which is very numerous, points out their places of abode and gives the most circumstantial and exact detail of their features, their stature and the several qualifications for which they are remarkable.'

A German physicist by the name of Georg Christoph Lichtenberg who visited London in 1772 also noted the brazen behaviour of the London whores: 'Before you know where you are a pretty, nicely dressed miss will take you by the hand, "Come my lord, come along, let us drink a glass together," or, "I'll go with you, if you please."'

In the same year he wrote: 'It is said that voluptuousness, evil and debauchery have never been so rampant in London as they are at present. Every ten yards one is beset even by children of twelve years old. Often they seize hold of you in such a fashion of which I can give you the best notion by the fact that I say nothing about it [...] I cannot understand why no one has tried to put an end to this evil.'

Twelve had been regarded as the age of consent for some 500 years and even younger children were involved in the sex trade. The concept of paedophilia as 'evil' just did not arise and there are stories of girls as young as eight years old being made available for sale by their needy mothers. In 1792 F.W. Schütz, another visitor from Germany, observed: 'The shamelessness of the children who, with the grown-ups, roamed the streets and offered their services to passers-by. Usually, a crowd of female creatures stand in front of the theatres, amongst whom may be found children of nine or ten years, the best evidence of moral depravity in London. In general, the English nation oversteps all others in immorality, and the abuses which come to light through addiction to debauchery are unbelievable.'

Half a century earlier a fellow-German called Zacharias Conrad von Uffenbach visited Oxford and Cambridge and stayed in London, commenting that at Cuper's Gardens there were 'disgraceful goings on. Near it is a tavern where men drink and find occasion for the devil's own work.' Well, men drinking in taverns and behaving badly is not exactly earth-shattering. Another German, Karl Philipp Moritz, had been born in September 1756 and came to London when he was twenty-five. Writing in 1782, in his work *Travels in England*, he had this to say about Ranelagh Gardens: 'At length I arrived at Ranelagh; and having paid my half-crown on entrance, I soon enquired for the garden door, and it was readily shown to me; when, to my infinite astonishment, I found myself in a poor, mean-looking, and ill-lighted garden, where I met but few people. I had not been here long before I was accosted by a young lady, who also was walking there, and who, without ceremony, offered me her arm, asking me why I walked thus solitarily?'

Of Vauxhall Gardens he said: 'I supped here with Mr. S——r, and the secretary of the Prussian ambassador, besides a few other gentlemen from Berlin; but what most astonished me was the boldness of the women of the town, who often rushed in upon us by half dozens, and in the most shameless manner importuned us for wine, for themselves and their followers. Our gentlemen thought it either unwise, unkind, or unsafe, to refuse them so small a boon altogether.'

The comments are a reminder that prostitutes could be found in all the main public spaces in London, openly plying their trade and accosting passing males. Some places, such as the watering hole known as Bagnigge Wells (Camden), were notorious as pick-up joints. Others, such as Ranelagh and Vauxhall, had a perfectly respectable clientele, but this was combined with a particularly seedy reputation on account of the harlots, pick-pockets and tricksters who also frequented them. Here, dukes and duchesses might be seen promenading just yards away from the most brazen of whores.

The openness of the sex scene amazed Joseph Baretti, an Italian literary critic and writer who visited London in the middle decades of the century. He called London 'a sink of vice' after a prostitute asked him for a glass of wine while he was visiting the Haymarket. He rejected her overtures, so she boxed him hard around his genitals. Baretti traded blows and became involved with three of her bullies, saying later in Court that: 'I was a Frenchman in their opinion, which made me apprehensive I must expect no favour or protection, but all outrage and blows.'

One of the men died from wounds inflicted by Baretti's fruit knife. He was tried for murder but acquitted on the grounds of self-defence, suggesting that British justice was kinder to foreigners than Baretti was to the street walkers he encountered. His defence was helped by the fact that the judge and one of the witnesses volunteered that they too had been accosted by whores in the Haymarket.

These are all comments made by men. It is also interesting to read the accounts of Sophie von la Roche, who visited London and describes a visit to the theatre: 'The box next to ours was occupied by eight so-called light girls, all with fine, blooming figures well dressed and true to their name, the most obvious gaiety in their eyes and faces. Not one of them looked older than twenty, and everyone so made that the best father or husband would be proud of having a virtuous daughter or wife with such stature and good features. [They were of course all prostitutes, no doubt looking for custom after the play finished].' La Roche continued: 'We were sorry to think that Mr Archenholz had counted fifty thousand of these surely unhappy creatures.'

She was referring to Johann Wilhelm Daniel von Archenholz, a German visitor to London in 1780. He spoke at length about prostitution in the city: 'So soon as it becomes dark these girls, well turned out, in all seasons flood the principal streets and squares of the town …. [At midnight] the old wretches, of fifty or sixty years of age, descend from their garrets, and attack the intoxicated passengers, who are often prevailed upon to satisfy their passions in the open street.'

He went on to say:

Many go on the man-hunt in borrowed clothes which they hire by the day from the matrons, who for safety's sake pay another woman to follow the huntress continuously on foot in order to see that she does not run away with the clothes. If the girl makes no capture and comes home without money, she will be ill-treated and must go hungry. They therefore accost passers-by and take them either home or to taverns. They can be seen standing in groups. The best class of prostitutes, who live independently, are content to go on their way 'til they are spoken to.

He had identified an important point about the eighteenth-century sex trade: workers wanted to appear as classy and well-dressed as they could, because they could charge high-end prices. Whores aspired to dress like duchesses. They were the fashionistas of the day and to that end were prepared to sign promissory notes at exorbitant rates of interest, in favour of the madam responsible for them, even though they were in effect committing themselves to a contract from which there was no escape. Few would ever earn enough to pay for the clothes they wore, but that did not stop them trying.

Archenholz also identified just how important prostitution was to the economy of London. It underpinned its whole prosperity: from the shops that supplied the fine gowns to the tavern owners who rented out rooms; from the purveyors of luxury goods to the owners of theatres where the leading courtesans rented boxes for the whole season in order to see and be seen. Without prostitution, he opined:

London would soon be depopulated; the melancholy of the English would become intolerable; the fine arts would be frightened away; one half of the inhabitants would be deprived of subsistence, and that superb metropolis converted into a sad and frightful desert. If any proofs are wanting, enter the shops of the citizens and ask them who are their best customers and who pay them the most regularly? They will immediately answer that they are the unfortunate women who deny themselves almost the necessities of life to purchase fine clothes and spend in one moment the whole gains of a week. Without them, the theatres would be empty: they not only repair to all public places in crowds, but draw after them thousands of young men, who frequent these places merely to see and converse with them.

But if the 'Harlot pound' brought prosperity to the capital it also meant a link between that prosperity and criminality and disease. Whoring and thieving were inextricably linked, as borne out by the records of criminal trials such as appear in the Newgate Calendar and the records of the Old Bailey. These include many cases where gold watches were stolen, or wallets lifted and pockets picked, by light-fingered whores. But above all, the success of the flourishing sex market meant disease, especially venereal disease, which spread throughout all classes and affected men and women of all ages, rank and status.

Archenholz estimated that there were 30,000 prostitutes in just the one London district of Marylebone, and that 1,700 of these were women in high keeping, in other words, installed in elegant premises by their lover and paid an annuity. 'These live very well, and without ever being disturbed by the magistrates.' His comment echoed a distinction – a type of whoring gradation – described in a book published in 1758 entitled *A Congratulatory Epistle from a Reformed Rake to John F...g Esq upon the new scheme of reforming prostitutes*. It listed ten different classifications of whores, starting with the most genteel, and working down through to the most miserable of sluts.

Looking at each category in turn:

1. **Women of Fashion, who intrigue**. This classification covered bored wives, perhaps married into the aristocracy, who felt sufficiently liberated to have multiple affairs simply because they wanted love, and sex, and could not find it within marriage. As they did not 'sell' sex they cannot really be classed as prostitutes.
2. **Demi-reps**. Girls of a dubious reputation were called demi-reps, short for demi-reputation. They would not have 'lived in' at the brothel or seraglio, but would have been brought in when customers required their services.
3. **Good-natured girls**. These were the unmarried women who would have sex with their admirers in return for a good meal and an evening's entertainment.
4. **Kept mistresses**. An example would be a courtesan paid an annuity, or provided with a house, by a man who was not her husband, and who would be available for sexual favours although not necessarily on an exclusive basis. In France these kept women were known as '*dames entretenues*', and the practice of keeping a mistress was termed '*la galanterie*'. In England, a whole new language developed in line with the French; men were no longer adulterers, they were 'gallants' and 'affairs' became 'intrigues'.
5. **Ladies of Pleasure**. These would be attractive, well-spoken prostitutes able to discuss current affairs with their admirers, perhaps play a musical instrument, and who would live in lodgings or high-class brothels.

6. **Whores**. Living in downmarket brothels, operating from bagnios, or making a living by picking up custom in the taverns and theatres such as the ones around Covent Garden.
7. **Park-walkers**. These would attract custom by walking through parks such as Ranelagh and New Spring Gardens (later Vauxhall Gardens). Well-dressed, they would attract male attention by a touch on the elbow or a provocative tilt of a fan.
8. **Street-walkers**. Openly accosting men in the street, and either servicing their clients in public places, (when they might be termed 'threepenny stand-ups') or in garrets or in rooms above taverns.
9. **Bunters**. These were the diseased whores, the lowest of the low. Unclean, often physically scarred by mercury poison and open syphilitic sores, bunters would be found near the docks, willing to exchange their favours for the price of a drink.
10. **Bulk mongers**. Homeless beggars, living rough and often in the final stages of disease.

The same book goes on to urge readers to accept that the higher-class sex-workers were just as likely to corrupt the morals of the nation as the lowly street-walker:

> If low, mean, Whores are a Bane to Society, by debauching the Morals, as well as Bodies, of Apprentices, and Lads scarce come to the Age of Puberty; if they frequently infect them with venereal Complaints, which almost as often terminate in as fatal Consequences; if they sometimes urge these youths to unwarrantable Practices for supporting their Extravagance in Gin; do not those in a more dazzling Situation produce still worse Consequences, by as much as they are above the others? Are not youths of good Family and Fortune seduced by these shining Harlots, who more frequently than their Inferiors in Rank, propagate the Species of an inveterate Clap, or a Sound-pox?

These tens of thousands of brazen minxes were not necessarily earning their living from full-time prostitution; they might be badly-paid milliners seeking to make a few pounds on the side. Incidentally, the word 'milliner' was used as a euphemism for a prostitute. In the same way, the word 'actress' was synonymous with a woman willing to offer her services after the stage curtains closed, and the area around the theatres in Drury Lane at Covent Garden became the centre of a burgeoning sex trade. They may have been servant girls who occasionally made a few shillings satisfying the whims of their randy employers. They may have been women who had no other means of avoiding starvation while seeking new employment. They may have been 'good time girls' who enjoyed sex and who were very happy to be paid for something they found pleasurable. And, of course, many were vulnerable young girls, seduced or raped and then abandoned to their fate.

Daniel Defoe, writing in 1725, was certainly of the view that young servant girls made up the majority of London prostitutes, and that they took to prostitution when they were unemployed, as a way of supporting themselves. 'This is the reason why our streets are swarming with strumpets. Thus many of them rove from place to place, from bawdy-house to service, and from service to bawdy-house again.'

The numbers are staggering, although estimates varied: one report in 1758 estimated that there were 62,500 whores plying their trade in London. By 1839 Michael Ryan was claiming in his book, *Prostitution in London, with a comparative view of that of Paris and New York*, that there were then about 80,000 prostitutes operating out of 5,000 brothels in the London metropolis. He also gives a figure of 400 full-time 'procurers' engaged in London in kidnapping young children for sale into the sex trade, with orphanages providing a constant supply of newcomers. Girls as young as eight or nine were lured into prostitution by a trade desperate for virgin newcomers.

What would be surprising to modern eyes is how open the sex trade was. This was no coy placement of 'business cards' in the corner of shop windows or left behind the bar in popular taverns: the trade was obvious and omnipresent and was even celebrated and promoted in trade directories such as the famous *Harris's List*, or to give it its full title, *Harris's List of Covent-Garden Ladies, or Man of Pleasure's Kalendar*, which first appeared in 1757 and was published annually throughout the thirty-eight-year period up to 1795. Armed with it, a visitor to London could take his pick of prostitutes to visit in the Covent Garden area. It gave their addresses, their age, their specialisms and their price: something which, in our own age, would be hard to envisage even on Facebook or Twitter.

All of these comments relate to London, and certainly do not mean that these scenes were replicated elsewhere. Indeed, there was nowhere else like London. It was not just that it was the largest city in the Western world, with over a million people crowded into the metropolis, making it considerably larger than Paris. In 1700 the other cities in England measured their populations in tens of thousands, not hundreds of thousands. Yes, there were port cities such as Bristol where prostitutes plied their trade, but nowhere as openly or on such a vast scale as in London. The capital city was a magnet, drawing people from all over the country, and particularly from Ireland, lured by tales of wealth, if not pavements paved with gold. This influx meant that many newcomers had no family support network; and no one to criticise or pass judgement.

As the century developed the rural poor drifted into the growing cities such as Birmingham, Manchester and Liverpool, seeking employment in factories and living in conditions which were often appalling. For many youngsters, destitution and prostitution went hand in hand, and all of these cities saw an unprecedented rise in very public displays of immorality. It was brazen, blatant and born out of desperation. Towns and cities north of the border were not immune from the spread of prostitution. The 'trade list', known as Rangers Impartial List, suggests that there were as few as half a dozen brothels in Edinburgh in 1763, but over 100 just twenty years later. The list gave colourful details of some sixty-six of the city's leading sex workers, described as 'nymphs' or 'worshippers of Venus'. Names, ages and addresses were given, as well as explicit details of the specialities on offer.

Elsewhere, in the villages and small towns, 'everyone knew everyone'. Here, away from the capital, people were quick to pass judgement and adulterers or couples 'living in sin' could find themselves subjected to a custom called 'rough music'. Wife-beaters, nagging scolds, unmarried mothers and others behaving in what was regarded as a shameful manner were all vulnerable targets of the crowd's derision. Villagers would walk from their own homes noisily banging pots and pans and make a cacophony outside the home of the misbehaving couple. Known variously as a 'charivari', or a 'skimmington', or as 'stang riding', the mob would sometimes drag the perceived wrongdoer from the house, and either pelt him or her, or dunk the miscreant in the village pond.

No such moral outrage was seen in London and one part of the capital was more extreme than any other: Covent Garden. This was the centre of the sex trade, an area described by the magistrate Sir John Fielding as 'the great square of Venus'. He went on to say: 'One would imagine that all the prostitutes in the kingdom had picked upon that blessed neighbourhood for a general rendezvous, for here are lewd women enough to fill a mighty colony, and [...] here is a great variety of open houses, whose principal employment is to minister incitement to lusty rakes and shameless prostitutes. These and the taverns afford ample supply of provision for the flesh, while others abound for the consummation of desires which are thus decided. For this design, the bagnios and lodging houses are near at hand.'

Sir John's elder half-brother was the playwright Henry Fielding, author of that boisterous romp through eighteenth-century England, *Tom Jones*. Henry had strong views on prostitution, commenting: 'Prostitutes are the lowest and meanest, so are they the basest, vilest, and wickedest of all Creatures. It is a trite Observation, that when a Woman quits her Modesty, she discards with it every other Virtue.'

This comment highlights the hypocrisy of the Georgians. They may have been much more honest and open about sex, but that did not mean that 'respectable' society accepted prostitutes. They were feted and praised on their own turf, but they were never welcome in the drawing rooms of the gentlemen who paid for their services. A reminder of this is that when Elizabeth Armistead, one of the most famous courtesans of the age, with a glittering clientele that included princes, dukes and lords by the score, settled down and married the politician Charles James Fox she insisted that the marriage be kept secret for seven years. She was afraid that the relationship would damage her husband's political career.

Oddly, there were no such concerns when the prostitute Nancy Parsons took up with the Duke of Grafton, prime minister of the day. He had separated from his wife and was happy to install his mistress in her place, to the extent that Nancy hosted dinner parties, and offered her opinion on political matters. Their conduct appeared scandalous to many, with the Tête-à-tête column of *Town & Country Magazine* commenting, 'She presides constantly at his sumptuous table, and does the honours with an ease and elegance, that the first nobility in the kingdom are compelled to admire.' The relationship did not last, and Nancy went on to marry Viscount Maynard. The wag Horace Walpole reflected that she 'deserved a peerage as much as many that have got them lately.'

Prostitutes generated a huge number of words describing them and their activities, as shown in a dictionary produced by Francis Grose and first published in 1785. Here are just a few:

Bat: A low whore; so called from moving out like bats in the dusk of the evening.
Biter: A lascivious, rampant wench.
Bunter: A low, dirty prostitute; half whore and half beggar.
A Hedge whore: An itinerant harlot, who bilks the bagnios and bawdy-houses by disposing of her favours on the wayside, under a hedge; a low beggarly prostitute.
Hoydon: A romping girl.
An Impure: A term for a lady of easy virtue.
One of us/one of my cousins: A woman of the town, a harlot.
Quean: A slut, or worthless woman, a strumpet.
Public ledger: A prostitute, because, like that paper, she is open to all parties.
Punk: A whore, also a soldier's trull.
A female screw: A common prostitute.
A Flash mollisher: A low-class whore.
Squirrel: A prostitute, because she, like that animal, covers her back with her tail.
Star gazer: A hedge whore.
Three-penny upright: A retailer of love, who, for the sum mentioned, dispenses her favours standing against a wall.
Trumpery: An old whore, or goods of no value; rubbish.
Unfortunate women: Prostitutes, so termed by the virtuous and compassionate of their own sex.
Woman of the town, or Woman of pleasure: A prostitute.

Perhaps the most interesting insight into London morality was provided by the now-infamous Casanova, who visited the city in June 1763. Using the name 'Jacques Casanova de Seingalt' or sometimes the 'Chevalier de Seingalt', he was never a 'wham, bam, thank you Ma'm' type of lover. For him the chase, the seduction, was everything. Casanova attracted great interest from the press when he put an advertisement in his window offering rent-free accommodation to any 'attractive young lady' willing to offer her services in lieu of rent. He interviewed numerous applicants before settling on 'Mistress Pauline'. The arrangement was never exclusive on his part and he describes being recommended by Lord Pembroke to try one of the girls on offer at a particular public house, the Staven Tavern.

Once there, he hired a private room and asked the publican to find a pretty girl. In his words, 'a girl of herculean proportions' soon entered the room.

> "Sir," said I, "I don't like the looks of this girl."
>
> "Give her a shilling and send her away. We don't trouble ourselves about ceremonies in London," replied the publican. This put me at my ease, so I paid my shilling and called for a prettier wench. The second was worse than the first, and I sent her away, and ten others after her, while I could see that my fastidiousness amused the landlord immensely. "I'll see no more girls," said I at last, "let me have a good dinner."

Twelve shillings poorer, he later castigated Lord Pembroke for his duff recommendation, only to be told that the mistake was in not asking for a particular girl by name. He returned with a list of names, but was just as disappointed the second time around.

However, if the great lothario was unimpressed with English beauty, he certainly was poleaxed by the charms of Marianne de Charpillon, a French-born courtesan living in Denmark Street on the borders of St Giles. She was a seventeen-year-old living with her Swiss mother, grandmother and aunts. Unknown to Casanova, they made a good living fleecing rich men of their money. From their first meeting, Marianne drew him on, encouraging him to buy expensive presents for her and hinting at pleasures to come. But no matter how much money he spent she refused to have sex with him. Eventually he got so fed up with her wiles that he tried to use force, and Marianne promptly had him arrested. It was alleged that he took his revenge by teaching a parrot to say, 'Miss Charpillon is more of a whore than her mother,' and putting it on display in the City's Royal Exchange.

It was a novel experience for the great lover, to be rejected, and by a whore of all people. His confidence at a low ebb, and apparently weakened by an attack of the pox, he left England and never came back.

Paying the price for love...

Chapter 3

How Royalty and the Rich Behaved

In the eighteenth century there was certainly one law for the rich and another for the poor, and more particularly one set of behaviour accepted for royalty and anyone with a title, and another for the general public. For the royals and the aristocracy marriage meant one thing and one thing only: begetting a legitimate male heir so that the title could be preserved. It meant that marriage was looked upon as a dynastic necessity, and 'wife material' meant someone who would be good breeding stock: healthy, pure and preferably rich. Sex within such a marriage was there in order to produce a healthy baby. And having achieved that, the husband would then turn to his mistress for a totally different sort of relationship; one where sex was for fun.

Wouski – a Gillray caricature showing Prince William sharing a hammock with a Jamaican prostitute.

The introductory statement to the marriage vows in the Anglican Book of Common Prayer, with origins dating back to Thomas Cranmer in 1552, starts off with the words, 'marriage was instituted for the procreation of children, as a remedy against sin and to avoid fornication.' Well, to the average earl, marquis or duke, he was happy to go along with the first bit, but rather lost interest in the rest of the sentence. A man with a title considered it perfectly normal to keep a mistress, often a succession of mistresses, and if money permitted, a positive collection of young ladies willing to indulge his every whim. And if they wanted an example of behaviour to follow, they needed to look no further than the reigning monarch. Or, to be more accurate, any of the reigning monarchs except King George III. He alone amongst all his family was a one-woman man, siring fifteen children by his wife, Charlotte of Mecklenburg-Strelitz. There may have been whispers of an earlier affair, and reputed marriage, involving a 'Fair Quaker from Cheltenham', but there is no proof of any such liaison, and certainly no suggestion of an affair after he and Queen Charlotte were married in 1761. As for others in his family, starting off with his great grandfather, the first King George; well, they weren't exactly role models for fidelity in marriage.

George I

When Georg Ludwig, ruler of the Duchy and Electorate of Brunswick-Lüneburg, came to England in 1714 to be crowned monarch, he did so minus his wife. There was a good reason for this: she was locked up in a castle back in Hanover, a prisoner for over thirty years.

By way of background, the Elector had married his first cousin, Sophia Dorothea, in 1682. It was not exactly a love match. She referred to him as 'pig snout' and begged not to be forced to go through with the marriage. For his part George preferred the company of his mistress, Melusine von der Schulenburg, but George and his wife nevertheless had two children, a boy and a girl. The royal couple drifted apart, and in the case of Sophia Dorothea, she embarked on an affair with the Swedish count, Philip Christoph von Königsmarck. Her husband's family were outraged and in 1694 arranged for the count to be murdered, possibly with the knowledge of George. He then divorced his wife on the grounds of her desertion and she was locked up for the rest of her life. George, meanwhile, had three children by his mistress, Melusine, and brought her with him when he came to England in 1714.

He also brought with him a woman believed to have been the daughter of his father's mistress. She was nicknamed 'The Elephant', to differentiate her from Melusine, known as 'The Maypole'. Maybe it was all part of the xenophobia on the part of the English courtiers, one of whom (Lord Chesterfield) said of the new king that he 'rejects no woman so long as she is very willing, very fat, and has great breasts'. The king was therefore rumoured to be having a sexual relationship with The Elephant, i.e. his illegitimate half-sister, whose real name was Sophia von Kielmansegg. The royal family vehemently denied any improper relationship, but the British public were very willing to suspect incest. Describing a childhood encounter with The Elephant, Horace Walpole recalled:

> being terrified at her enormous figure [...] two fierce black eyes, large and rolling beneath two lofty arched eyebrows, two acres of cheeks spread with crimson, an ocean of neck that overflowed and was not distinguished from the lower part of her body, and no part restrained by stays; no wonder that a child dreaded such an ogress, and that the mob of London were highly diverted at the importation of so uncommon a seraglio! [...] indeed nothing could be grosser than the ribaldry that was vomited out in lampoons, libels, and every channel of abuse, against the sovereign and the new court, and chaunted even in their hearing about the public streets.

Sophia was the complete opposite of the willowy Maypole, who Horace Walpole termed 'long and emaciated.' Melusine, or The Maypole, was loathed by the English court. She was hated for being dull and stupid, for having appalling dress-sense, for being avaricious, and for condoning incest (by sharing the king's bed with his half-sister). She must have had something going for her though, since the king kept her as his mistress for almost forty years, and during that time she became an invaluable intermediary between the king and his ministers. The king gave her the title of Duchess of Kendal and she grew rich on the sale of appointments, and incurred the wrath of Grub Street hacks who resented her meddling in British politics. As Robert Walpole remarked, she was 'as much Queen of England as any ever was [...] he [George I] did everything by her'. Above all though, she and The Elephant were closely linked with the scandal of the stock market crash in 1720, known as 'The South Sea Bubble'. The scandal did not prevent Sophia becoming Countess of Leinster in 1721, and then the Countess of Darlington and Baroness Brentford a year later. She died in 1725 and was buried in Westminster Abbey. Melusine, who went by an alternative nickname of 'The Scarecrow' in Germany and 'The Goose' in Scotland, died in 1743.

King George moved on to a new mistress – his first English one – a woman by the name of Anna Brett. Horace Walpole refers to her as being 'very handsome, but dark enough by her eyes, complexion, and hair, for a Spanish beauty.' The aristocracy was horrified to hear the rumour that she was to be elevated to the rank of countess, since Mistress Brett (as she was derogatively called) was the daughter of a mere colonel with an infamous mother. No sooner had she started throwing her weight about at the palace, making alterations and rubbing up The Maypole the wrong way, than news of the death of the king came through. She never did get her hands on a ducal coronet, and she disappeared from court and into obscurity.

George II

Here was a man who seems almost half-hearted in his pursuit of mistresses. He married Caroline of Ansbach in 1705 when he was twenty-two. They went on to have eight children during their thirty-two-year marriage, and throughout that time George also enjoyed the company of a succession of mistresses. But whereas you can hardly imagine Charles II sitting down in the evening to play cards with Nell Gwynn, that is exactly what George II was apt to do with his mistress, Henrietta Howard, who later became Countess of Suffolk. Another mistress was Amalie von Wallmoden. She happened to be the niece of The Maypole, his father's mistress, so it really was a case of keeping things in the family.

She is believed to have had at least one illegitimate child by the king, and was awarded the title of Countess of Yarmouth for her troubles. George appears to have been genuinely fond of his wife and always kept her in the picture about his mistresses, and when Caroline lay dying and urged him to remarry, he apparently replied that he would not, and that he would have a mistress instead. When it was his turn to die, he left express instructions that he was to be buried in Westminster Abbey, immediately adjacent to his wife's body, and for the dividing wall between the two burial plots to be removed so that their bones would intermingle in death. Theirs was clearly a loving relationship, and the existence of the odd mistress or two looks more like keeping up appearances than any serious attempt at licentiousness and debauchery.

George III

Were it not for the sexual incontinence of his siblings and his son, you would think that the Georgians under Farmer George had developed a taste for abstinence and self-control. Perhaps, having fathered fifteen children, he simply could not be bothered, but what George III lacked in variety was certainly made up for by other members of the family.

The king's younger sister was Caroline Matilda. She had been married at fifteen by proxy to a man she had never met; a drunken, whoring, Danish king by the name of Christian VII, and was stuck in a foreign court where she didn't speak the language and knew nothing of their customs. Her husband declined to stop visiting the local brothels, and in all probability gave her a nasty case of the pox as a result. She sought treatment from a Dr Struensee, who offered her rather more than just a cure. They became lovers, even though he was nearly twice her age, probably with the full knowledge and connivance of the king. She had a child by her lover, but in due course pressure from disgruntled courtiers forced the mentally unstable king to take action against the happy pair. The ambitious but foolish doctor was tortured into making a confession, and was executed in 1772. The queen was tried for adultery, convicted, divorced, sent into exile, caught scarlet fever, and was dead at the age of twenty-three. Not once did her brother, George III, offer any sympathy or support. On hearing of her death, the king even barred her body from being returned for burial in Westminster Abbey. She had brought disgrace to the family.

It was, in part, a classic example of Georgian double standards: a woman could not get away with behaviour which for a man was perfectly acceptable. But it also shows that King George III recognized something which others in his family did not: that the royal family should be setting an example to the nation, and that appearances mattered. For that reason, he must have been mortified by the actions of his brother, Prince Henry, the Duke of Cumberland.

As already mentioned, the duke was caught *in flagrante* with the wife of Lord Grosvenor in 1769. The duke brought an action alleging criminal conversation (in effect, adultery) against the prince and was awarded damages of £10,000, plus legal costs of some £3,000, all of which had to be paid out of the royal purse. These damages were payable despite the undeniable fact that Lord Grosvenor had been the first to break the marriage vows and was a known habitué of many of the local brothels. More humiliatingly for the royal family, the court case attracted a huge amount of interest from the press. Evidence from royal servants revealed minute details about royal lifestyles: what time the duke rose, where he took breakfast, what time he visited his club and so on, bringing these facts into the public domain. Within days of the verdict, the public could buy books containing copies of the statements made in court, read the intimate letters between the parties, and make themselves familiar with all the salacious details. Lady Grosvenor became a social outcast, but did at least get an allowance of £1,200 a year from her husband. The Duke of Grosvenor carried on whoring and gambling prodigiously, and when he died in 1801 he had debts equivalent to eight million pounds.

As for the king's brother, Henry went off and married Anne Horton, a widow known to have been notoriously free with her favours. King George was horrified at the union, and promptly asked Parliament to pass the Royal Marriages Act, stating that any marriage by a member of the royal family was invalid unless it was made with the monarch's approval. This was to have serious consequences for many of the king's children, because they ended up in unions that were contrary to the provisions of the Royal Marriages Act. As a result, their offspring were royal bastards, unable to claim their place in the line of succession.

The Prince of Wales (later, the Prince Regent and later still, George IV)

Here was a man who never did things by halves. He never felt constrained by what the public might think and never felt that sexual abstinence was in any way necessary or even advisable. The result was a constant stream of criticism, which in turn developed into outright loathing. In part this was linked to his extravagance and wastefulness with public money, in part it was linked to the way he treated his wife, the unloved Queen Caroline, and in part because of his reputation as 'the randy Regent'. The result was that when he died, in 1827, *The Times* newspaper reported that 'there never was an individual less regretted by his fellow-creatures than this deceased king.'

The attitude of the Prince Regent towards sex, especially extramarital sex, speaks volumes about how the sexual mores of the nation had moved on during the eighteenth century. What was central to his life was not the family, but the pursuit of pleasure. His hedonistic lifestyle shocked the public and led to the pendulum-swing heralded by the arrival on the throne of the young Queen Victoria. Throughout his adult life his peccadilloes and his libidinous behaviour were exposed to public scrutiny, with caricaturists such as James Gillray and father-and-son, Isaac and George Cruikshank, having an absolute field day. Indeed, when the Prince Regent became king in 1820 he was happy to offer a bribe of £100 to George Cruikshank in return for a promise 'not to caricature His Majesty in any immoral situation'.

There was plenty for the satirists to take aim at: the determination of the young Prince of Wales to seduce the impecunious actress Mary Robinson (by promising her a 'signing-on' fee of £20,000); his willingness to dump her without warning when he took up with the courtesan Grace Dalrymple Elliott; his affair with Viscountess Melbourne; and, in December 1785, his rumoured marriage to Maria Fitzherbert, a twice-married Roman Catholic, contrary to the provisions of the Royal Marriages Act. There were innumerable other affairs throughout this 'marriage' plus a considerable number of 'extra-curricular activities' in local brothels and seraglios. There was also a well-publicised affair with the charming and curvaceous Elizabeth Armistead. Then came the marriage, somewhat forced on him because of the parlous state of his finances, to Caroline of Brunswick. When he met her, George was appalled: he found her repulsive and ugly. Worse, she was unwashed, and had bad body odour. He got so drunk on his wedding night that he collapsed insensible in the fireplace, but in due course he did his duty, got her pregnant, and vowed never to have anything further to do with her.

Caroline travelled through Europe with her presumed lover, an Italian commoner called Bertolomeo Pergami. The Prince Regent was outraged and wanted a divorce, but the more he tried to dig up evidence against his wife the more obvious it was that the public would not stomach such hypocrisy. They knew all about his affair with Frances, Lady Jersey, daughter of an Irish Bishop and by then an attractive forty-one-year old married grandmother. They knew too about Isabella, Lady Hertford, who was the Prince's mistress from 1807 to 1819, and who was then succeeded as the prince's favourite by Elizabeth, Marchioness Conyngham. Each mistress appeared to be even stouter than the last. By then the loathing against the Prince Regent was considerable, and was increased still further when he became king and announced that Caroline would not be permitted to attend the coronation in Westminster Abbey in 1821. The fact that the queen died just a few days later – possibly of stomach cancer – merely added to a popular belief that she had been poisoned. George IV reigned for ten years in his own right, largely as a recluse suffering from painfully swollen limbs, and from laudanum addiction.

William IV

When George IV was succeeded to the British throne in 1827 by his brother, William, it merely underlined the sexual freedom enjoyed by the royals. As the Duke of Clarence, William had earned the nickname of 'the sailor king' because of his time serving as an officer in the Royal Navy. More accurately, he spent his time touring all the brothels on the island of Jamaica. Subsequently, he took up with the actress Dorothea Jordan and she became the prince's mistress for twenty-one years, producing ten children by him, all basking under the surname of FitzClarence. Then one day William realized that he needed to be married if he was ever to become king, so in 1811 he chucked her out with a miserly allowance, and instead married a German princess. Dorothea was left destitute, fled to France to avoid her creditors, but died in abject poverty in 1816. William had no legitimate children and when he died in 1837 the crown passed to his niece, Princess Victoria. Time for the pendulum to swing back in favour of family values!

So, what is to be made of these royal shenanigans? They certainly show a cynical disregard for marriage vows and a willingness to be quite open about affairs. The example they set was eagerly followed by many members of the nobility, especially the men, who were more than willing to adopt double standards. But, just to state the obvious, not every aristocratic woman in the Georgian era stayed at home meekly waiting for her husband to return. As likely as not she was out looking for love. The difference was that society generally did not accept that she was entitled to do so.

Take the case of Georgiana Spencer, who was to become the Duchess of Devonshire. Married on her seventeenth birthday, she found herself unable to give the 5th duke a male heir. He maintained various adulterous relationships throughout the marriage and when Georgiana befriended Lady Elizabeth Foster ('Bess') the duke in effect hijacked the friendship by starting an affair with Bess. What was unusual, and scandalous at the time, was that this resulted in *a ménage à trois* in which Bess was living in the matrimonial home with the duke and duchess. There was much gossip and speculation as to whether there was a physical relationship between Georgiana and Bess; there was clearly a very strong emotional bond. Bess was never sold on the idea of one lover at a time, and had various affairs with other men, even while living as part of the duke's household. Over a period of some years her name was linked with Cardinal Ercole Consalvi, as well as John Sackville, 3rd Duke of Dorset, and also Count Axel von Fersen. Charles Lennox, 3rd Duke of Richmond, and Valentine Quin, 1st Earl of Dunraven and Mount-Earl were also believed to have been lovers. Basically, Bess managed to have her cake and eat it: she was, after all, already married, the mother of three sons, and was entirely dependent on the largesse of the duke.

Georgiana was not so fortunate. After sixteen years of marriage she gave birth to a legitimate son and in doing so some would regard her as having earned the right to have affairs of her own. In fact, she fell for the charms of Charles Grey, became pregnant by him, and thereby earned the wrath of her jealous husband. She was forced to hand over the resulting child to Grey's family, and was sent into exile in France for a number of years. When she returned, poor Georgiana never really recovered her position in society. She died at the age of forty-eight, with massive gambling debts, which fell to her husband to settle. The duke married Bess three years later, but died after two years, leaving Bess to lay claim to a number of property assets and to argue that her own illegitimate children by the duke should receive various benefits. All of this was contested by William Cavendish, the new 6th duke. He eventually paid her off. She died in Rome in March 1824.

Another high-profile case that captured the public imagination, and in which the woman in the centre eventually succeeded after a lengthy struggle and public condemnation, involved Lady Seymour Worsley. She had been a wealthy heiress, married at the age of twenty-one. Caught in a loveless marriage with Sir Richard Worsley, 7th Baronet of Appuldurcombe, she was an outrageous flirt. She liked London parties, not being shut away on the Isle of Wight while her husband pursued his political and military career. He wanted military precision, order, and a chance to spend his wife's not inconsiderable fortune in amassing what he hoped would be the country's finest collection of sculptures from ancient Greece. It is also likely that he got his kicks from looking through the keyhole and watching his young bride find an outlet for marital boredom with a succession of the baronet's friends. One such friend was a neighbour, George Bissett, and on one occasion the three of them went to the public baths, where Sir Richard happily assisted Bissett watch Lady Seymour undress through an open window. Lady Seymour and George Bissett became lovers and she gave birth to a daughter who was almost certainly fathered by Bissett. This did not seem to concern Sir Richard and he was happy to acknowledge the child as his own in order to avoid public scandal. But the news was soon to come out into the open, because Lady Seymour eloped with Bissett, spending four nights with him at the Royal Hotel at Pall Mall in London, only leaving the bedroom when they wanted the sheets changed.

The humiliated Sir Richard wanted revenge and set out to expose his wife's infidelity. Rather than divorce his wife – or even to ask for a formal separation – he decided to sue Bissett in the King's Bench Division for 'crim. con.' (Criminal Conversation) and sought damages of £20,000. The amount would have been enough to have destroyed Bissett, and was set so high because it was intended to reflect the fact that Bissett was a man in a position of trust (he was not just a neighbour and a friend, but also, shock horror, a junior officer in the same regiment as the baronet). He had abused that trust when he committed adultery with Lady Seymour and had thereby 'damaged' her.

At the trial it soon became apparent that it was not Bissett who had first 'damaged' her ladyship. Stories emerged that she was somewhat fast and loose when spreading her favours, and that there were, in fact, another twenty-six paramours in the background. Much of that was pure speculation – Lady Seymour only had to flash a smile in the direction of a passing male for the press to exaggerate the incident as a full-blown affair – but five of the alleged lovers were prepared to give evidence in support of Bissett's claim that he was not the first to 'damage the goods'.

One such witness was Viscount Deerhurst, who had been encountered by Sir Richard in his wife's bedchamber at four in the morning. He gave evidence admitting the encounter, but he declined to answer what he was doing there. More damning was the evidence from the staff at the Royal Hotel: there was only the one bed in the room which the lovers shared. Another witness was a Dr Osborne, who was called to explain the circumstances in which he had examined Lady Seymour. He claimed patient confidentiality, but then went on to say that Lady Seymour Worsley had consented to him disclosing that she had sought treatment for venereal disease. The press went into overdrive, and suggested that she had contracted the disease from the Duke of Montrose (also a witness in the trial).

To the gossip columnists this was manna from heaven: twenty-six lovers in addition to Bissett, plenty of juicy details and gossip, and a tale of a man who dishonourably absconded with another man's wife! She was portrayed as a nymphomaniac, with carnal desires so insatiable that it took dozens of men to satisfy her lust. And then there was the public baths incident. It was pointed out to the court that Sir Richard was a party to his own cuckolding. When Lord Mansfield addressed the jury before they withdrew to consider their verdict, he made it clear that the facts were not in dispute, stating: 'This Woman, for three or four years, has been prostituted with a variety of people; that is extremely clear, and extremely plain.' The jury did as they were directed, but instead of assessing damages at £20,000 they awarded the humiliating sum of just one shilling.

Lady Seymour became one of a group of 'fallen women' who met at an informal club known as the New Female Coterie. She survived on favours and occasional financial support from wealthy friends, but when Bissett got her pregnant again he deserted her for a younger lover. She swapped London for Paris, and found that the French were less censorious about her lifestyle. She got caught up in the aftermath of the French Revolution, and was trapped in Paris during the Terror. The baronet, who had spent the intervening twenty years building up his art collection, died in 1805. Sir Richard's death transformed Seymour's prospects: the fortune which she had brought into the marriage reverted to her. Now wealthy and living in Britain, she married a Frenchman and settled happily near Farnham in Surrey. When the Napoleonic Wars ended the couple moved to Paris, where she died in 1818.

What these cases show is that the newspapers of the day were preoccupied with stories about misbehaving aristocrats and randy royals. Trials were a wonderful opportunity for reporters to pander to an insatiable and voyeuristic appetite on the part of the public. If the stories showed 'excessive' female sexual desire, so much the better. The stories also reveal the way in which it was accepted that illegitimacy and venereal disease were an ever-present fact of life. They also show that a man could commit adultery and yet keep his place in society, whereas a woman could not. If an adulterous wife was legally separated from her husband she lived in a sort of limbo, her character stained. Only if her husband died or divorced her could she remarry and regain respectability.

'A peep into Lady W!!!!!y's seraglio' showing Lady Seymour Worsley and some of her twenty-seven lovers...

Chapter 4

Courtesans, Celebrity Whores and Fashionistas

It is worth looking at some of the women who made it to the top of the tree. These were the 'Toasts of the Town', the women who achieved a celebrity status, who dominated the fashion scene, and whose success and fame inspired many young girls to follow in their footsteps. Of course we need to remember that for every one who made it to the top, there were at least a thousand who remained out of the limelight, languishing in abject poverty and extreme ill-health. And perhaps another thousand more who were part-timers, drifting in and out of prostitution, hoping to make ends meet but never achieving fame or fortune. But for the lucky few, strutting their stuff across the London scene, they lived a life of unbelievable luxury.

Sally Salisbury from an engraving of 1723.

Sarah Pridden, aka Sally Salisbury c.1692–1724

Sarah, according to one rumour, had changed her name because she was told that she looked like the Duchess of Salisbury. She started off as an apprentice seamstress, but apparently moved on to selling pamphlets in the city of London. In fact, that was a 'front' for providing 'personal services' to schoolboys and apprentices in the area, charging half a crown a time.

She progressed to become one of the first celebrity whores of the eighteenth century, and boasted a number of dukes, Secretary of State Lord Bolingbroke, and even, it was rumoured, the future George II, as her clients. She had originally been the fourteen-year-old mistress of the loathsome Francis Charteris featured in Chapter 9, but moved on to a succession of well-connected admirers, largely thanks to her sparkling wit and good looks. She spent faster than she earned and was forever in debt, and on various occasions languished in debtors prisons. Memorably she was once released from jail because Judge Blagney, who was presiding over her case, was completely infatuated with her.

In 1722 she stabbed and wounded a lover in a fit of jealousy because she thought that he was two-timing her. He had apparently bought tickets for the opera, but was intending to take Sarah's sister as his companion, not her. The trial that followed the incident was a media sensation, attended by the great and the good, and was widely reported in the press where it was viewed as a crime of passion. She was found guilty and sentenced to a year's imprisonment. She was sent to Newgate Prison to serve her sentence but died after only nine months, probably of syphilis (officially, 'brain fever brought on by debauch'). Even in death her celebrity status continued, with two biographies coming out in 1723 under the titles of *The Genuine History of Mrs. Sarah Pridden, usually called Sally Salisbury, and Her Gallants*, and the *Authentic Memoirs of the Life, Intrigues and Adventures of the Celebrated Sally Salisbury*. Her legacy was to be remembered for her beauty, for her temper and for being a woman of passion. Even fifty years after her death a ditty appeared in print in The Sailor's Jester:

> Here flat on her back, but inactive at last,
> Poor Sally lies under grim death;
> Thro' the course of her vices she gallop'd so fast,
> No wonder she's now out of breath.

Sophia Baddeley 1745–1786

Another shooting star was Sophia Baddeley who, in her heyday, was regarded as being one of the most beautiful women of the century.

Certainly Lord Ancaster was known to have remarked that her beauty was 'absolutely one of the wonders of the age'. Her admirers included HRH the Duke of York, who gave her a lock of his hair as a memento.

There are very few portraits of her other than in stage costume. As an actress she was truly terrible, but the audiences absolutely adored her and she had a fine singing voice. She had married an impoverished actor when she was eighteen, but the marriage foundered, especially after her husband tried to persuade her to go to bed with a wealthy merchant who was keen to pay for her favours. They split up, and Sophia used her popularity and good looks to secure a succession of wealthy lovers. Her extravagance was simply staggering: she spent today's equivalent of £200 a day on hothouse flowers, and thousands a month on hats and linen. One year she spent the modern equivalent of a quarter of a million pounds on diamonds. A present from her protector, Lord Melbourne, for the equivalent of £3,000 would last her barely four days. She was an alcoholic and also a laudanum user, and was described by a contemporary as suffering from 'a dreadful and excessive indulgence in love, liquor, lust and laudanum.'

Her fall from grace was swift. After getting pregnant with an impecunious conman, she returned briefly to the stage, but at the age of forty-one, her looks and money gone, she died suddenly of consumption, or in other words tuberculosis. A year after her death her life story was published in six volumes by her lifelong friend, Elizabeth Steele, as *The Memoirs of Sophia Baddeley*.

Fanny Murray 1729–1788

Fanny had an unpromising start in life. She was born in Bath around 1729 to the wife of an itinerant musician called Rudman. Both parents were dead by the time she was twelve and she eked a living as a flower-seller on the streets of Bath near the Abbey and outside the Assembly Rooms. She was an attractive young girl and unfortunately she caught the eye of a philanderer called Jack Spencer. He was the grandson of Sarah, Duchess of Marlborough, and no doubt saw the seduction of a twelve-year-old orphan as a bit of fun. He had his wicked way with her, and promptly left. His place was taken by a captain in the army, but he too deserted her, leaving her at the mercy of all the unscrupulous rakes and pimps about town. Enter a rather strange hero; none other than the ageing roué Beau Nash, the Master of Ceremonies at the Assembly Rooms. No matter that at sixty-six he was over fifty years her senior, he invited her to become his mistress, and for a couple of years she was his devoted help-mate. He gave her polish and a taste for the good life, and in return, no doubt, she gave him a big smile on his face.

She then moved up to London, securing a place in *Harris's List* which described her as 'a new face [...] Perfectly sound in wind and limb. A fine Brown girl, rising nineteen next season. A good side-box piece, she will show well in the Flesh Market'.

She rocketed to fame and by the end of her teens was widely acknowledged as the 'Toast of the Town', so much so that she is widely credited as being the inspiration for Fanny Hill, the central character in John Cleland's *Memoirs of a Woman of Pleasure*, published in 1749. Fanny-mania took hold and she was always in the news. She became the mistress of John Montagu, the 4th Earl of Sandwich, and he introduced her to other members of the Hellfire Club, which met at Medmenham Abbey. Here, Fanny would take part in orgies in her capacity as a 'nun', which was the term given to females attending the club.

By the age of twenty-seven she had run up immense debts and was in dire straits. Her youthful good looks were fading, her creditors were pushing for payment, and her gallants deserted her in her hour of need. She was carted off to the sponging house (a temporary holding place for debtors) and her inevitable downward spiral into poverty and degradation must have been staring her in the face. But fortune favours the brave, and she decided to pen a letter to the son of the man who had first debauched her.

The young Mr Spencer was exceedingly honourable and generous, settling an annuity of £200 on Fanny. He also did her the great favour of introducing her to a friend of his, an actor called David Ross. The two fell in love, and to the amazement of everyone, got married. Fanny really had turned over a new leaf. She led a blameless married life for twenty years before dying at the age of forty-nine.

Nancy Parsons, aka Anne, Viscountess Maynard c.1735–1814/15

The daughter of a Bond Street tailor, as a teenager Nancy appears to have been drawn to prostitution, charging clients a guinea a time, and according to one of her boasts, was able to earn 100 guineas in a week, which is quite some work-rate. It is the equivalent of over £8,000 a week nowadays, or half a million pounds a year, with no PAYE, National Insurance or other deductions.

In her late teens she had married, but her husband quickly died and she was left earning a penny in the only way she knew: on her back. She slept her way up through society until she ended up in the bed of the 3rd Duke of Grafton, who just happened to be the first minister. By 1763 she had become his official mistress. The duke abandoned his wife, who in any event was busy having affairs of her own, and risked tarnishing his political career. Nancy even hosted dinner parties with him, or at least she did until he grew bored and started to look elsewhere. Meanwhile, Horace Walpole dismissed Nancy as 'one of the commonest creatures in London.'

It was an unusually public indiscretion on the part of the third duke, and one which was commented on in the *Town & Country Magazine*. In its Tête-à-Tête column, a regular gossip and scandal section, she was given the nickname of Annabella and it was reported: 'Annabella is now the happiest of her sex, attached to the most amiable man of the age, whose rank and influence raise her, in point of power, beyond many queens of the earth. Caressed by the highest, courted and adulated by all, her merit and shining abilities receive that applause that is justly due to them. There must have been many both in government and in society in general who were horrified at the turn of events.

By 1769 Nancy had moved on to become the mistress of the Duke of Dorset, but soon she set her sights on the 2nd Viscount Maynard. He was just twenty-four, whereas she was past her fortieth birthday, and no doubt keen to get a ring on her finger before age dulled her charms. She married her viscount in September 1776, and the couple went to live outside Naples in Italy. But her appetite got the better of her, and her particular 'seven-year itch' involved Francis Russell, fifth Duke of Bedford. He was just nineteen, and he joined the pair of them in a curious *ménage à trois* in Nice. Eventually she drifted apart from her husband – and her young lover – and led a solo existence in Italy and then France, dying near Paris in 1814 at the age of seventy-nine.

Kitty Fisher (born Catherine Fischer) c.1738–1767

When Nancy put down the crown as Toast of the Town, her place was taken immediately by young Kitty Fisher. She had probably been born in 1738, and although she did not live to see her thirtieth birthday, her career burned like a shooting star. She was considered beautiful and charming, and had her portrait painted by several members of the new Royal Academy, including nine times by its future president, Sir Joshua Reynolds. Originally a milliner by trade, she specialized in affairs with wealthy young men and quickly became an arbiter of fashion.

Readers of the book *Chrysal: or, The Adventures of a Guinea*, published in 1768, would instantly have recognized Kitty Fisher where she is described in one passage as being 'the most pretty extravagant, wicked little whore that ever flourished'. Her sexual allure and brazen behaviour captivated London, and at the height of her career she was charging a hundred guineas a night. Her lovers included Admiral Lord George Anson, in charge of the navy, as well as General John Ligonier, head of the British army. Then there was Edward, Duke of York, but he rather blotted his copybook by offering a paltry fifty pounds, and was promptly thrown out of bed. In 1763 she met Casanova, then on a visit to London. In his words: 'I was introduced to the illustrious Kitty Fisher, who was just beginning to be fashionable. She was magnificently dressed, and it is no exaggeration to say that she had on diamonds worth five hundred thousand francs. I was told that if I liked I might have her then and there. I did not care to do so, however, for, though charming, she could only speak English.'

Never one to miss the equivalent of a photo-opportunity (she loved to be seen, and was a self-publicist without equal) she took to riding in Hyde Park, and in their turn the public took to coming along to watch her ride by. One day she engineered a fall in front of a group of gallant soldiers. Cue a dramatic rescue of a damsel in distress, along with much thigh on display. Exit Kitty in a smart sedan chair which just happened to be waiting nearby. The press quickly reported the incident, with headlines saying that she was a 'fallen woman twice over'.

One of Kitty's conquests was Lord Coventry, who some years earlier had married Maria Gunning. Maria had come to England from Ireland with her equally glamorous sister in 1750, and both had used their famous looks to marry into the aristocracy. According to Giustiniana Wynne, an Anglo-Venetian writer and friend of Casanova, Kitty encountered Maria while out riding:

> The other day they ran into each other in the park and Lady Coventry asked Kitty the name of the dressmaker who had made her dress. Kitty Fisher answered she had better "ask Lord Coventry as he had given her the dress as a gift." The altercation continued with Lady Coventry calling her an impertinent woman, and Kitty replying that she would have to accept this insult because Maria became her "social superior" on marrying Lord Coventry, but she was going to marry a Lord herself just to be able to answer back.

Giustiniana went on to say of Kitty that 'She lives in the greatest possible splendour, spends twelve thousand pounds a year, and she is the first of her social class to employ liveried servants — she even has liveried chaise porters.'

This suggests that the feisty Kitty Fisher not only believed in ostentatious displays of wealth but was well aware that marriage could give her a status that notoriety could not. In the event, much to the amazement of the public, she announced that she was marrying an impecunious MP called Mr Norris. But ill-health was beginning to take its toll. Whether it was smallpox, or consumption, or the effect of ingesting lead from heavy make-up, her health deteriorated and her doting husband decided to take her to the Hot Wells in Bristol to 'take the waters' and effect a cure. She died on the journey and the heartbroken Mr Norris took her body home to Benenden and buried her in all of her finery, wearing her jewellery and her best gown. Her life story quickly appeared in print, but with little attempt at historical accuracy, and her name lives on today in the nursery rhyme:

> Lucy Locket lost her pocket,
> Kitty Fisher found it;
> But ne'er a penny was there in it,
> Except the binding round it.

A more accurate observation of her extraordinary career appears in a biography by the Edwardian writer Horace Bleackley, in his book *Ladies Fair and Frail*:

> To the historian the life of Kitty Fisher displays a curious picture of bygone morality, revealing the manners and customs of a robust age, before mankind had learned to hide their frailties from one another, when society went naked and was not ashamed. It was a period of hard living and plain speaking, when the Seventh Commandment was the least respected of all the ten, when *Harris's List of Covent Garden Ladies* was sold openly in public places, and a bagnio stood in every street [...] Like most human creatures, Kitty Fisher was a product of her age.

Nelly O'Brien c.1739–1768

An exact contemporary of Kitty was Nelly O'Brien. Little is known about her upbringing, but she shares the limelight with Kitty because she too was painted on more than one occasion by Sir Joshua Reynolds. Nelly had been a minor actress, and like many on the stage had used her skills to attract the attention of wealthy admirers. One was the naval hero Augustus Keppel (who later became an admiral and eventually a viscount). She moved on to become the mistress of the Second Viscount Bolingbroke, known to all as Bully, and who later went through a notorious divorce from his wife, Lady Diana Spencer, elder daughter of the Duke of Marlborough. Nelly gave birth to Bolingbroke's child in 1764 before drifting into an affair with Sackville Tufton, 8th Earl of the Isle of Thanet. She bore him two children. She presumably felt 'secure' as Tufton's mistress (he was unmarried) and so must have been devastated when the earl suddenly kicked her out of the home which he had provided for her, and announced that he was getting married. The announcement came at a time when Nancy was heavily pregnant. She miscarried, and died when complications set in, at the age of twenty-nine. If ever a life showed the downside of celebrity status, and its lack of security or permanence, it was that of Eleanor O'Brien.

Gertrude Mahon ('The Bird of Paradise') 1752–c.1808

Another Toast of the Town was a girl by the name of Gertrude Mahon. She was a veritable pocket Venus at just 49in tall. Her father had died when Gertrude was twelve and her mother, the Countess of Kerry, was more interested in pampering her cage birds and lap-dogs than in giving guidance to an impressionable daughter. She quickly became a wild child and at the age of seventeen fell head-over-heels for an itinerant Irish musician called Gilbreath Mahon. What little money he earned from fiddling, he lost at cards, but nothing would put off the coquettish little Gertrude. She eloped with him to Dover, hoping to get married in France, but her mother sent a pair of Bow Street Runners to intercept them. They were stopped, but the enterprising Gilbreath Mahon invited the posse to sit down for a libation, and promptly drank them both under the table before escaping into the night. The couple sailed off to France, got married, and within a year Gertrude had a daughter.

That was just about all she did get. Mr Mahon went off with another woman, leaving Gertrude penniless. She did what she had to do to survive: the 'Lilliputian seductress' used her charm, her brilliant complexion, her tiny frame and her dark eyes to entice a string of men into her bedroom.

Her love of bright clothing, and in particular her choice in millinery, made her a popular figure, never out of the limelight. Her hats earned her the nickname 'The Bird of Paradise'. She moved in with a dashing army officer called Captain John Turner, a man who was intent on squandering an inheritance of £50,000 as rapidly as possible. She helped him in his mission but had to move on rather swiftly when Turner realized that she was sharing her favours with his brother. She then paired up with a seventeen-year-old baronet called John Lade, and the *Morning Post* of 19 April 1777 gleefully reported that: 'The Bird of Paradise broke through the upper part of her cage two days ago, flew from her military keeper and perched on the shoulder of Sir John L…d as she was driving her phaeton and four through Knightsbridge, who carried her home to Park Place. The forsaken captain is disconsolate.'

In less than two years she decided that it was time to move on to pastures new. The good times, when she headed the demi-monde, lasted perhaps eleven years, but fame did not endure. She moved constantly around England, with a spell in Bath and another in Margate, before going to the continent, and then over to Ireland, with a succession of lovers. She was still appearing on stage into the 1790s, but by then the press had lost interest in her and when she died it was without trace or obituary.

Grace Elliott ('Dally the Tall') c.1754–1823

Grace Elliott had been born in around 1754. Her father was a prominent Scottish lawyer, but her parents split up before she was born and when she was eleven Grace was sent to a French convent to finish her education. She was witty, vivacious and sophisticated, as well as being regarded as good looking. She was also willowy and tall, and cut a most elegant figure. She elected to marry a very much older man, Dr John Elliott, who was fourteen years her senior. He was rich, dedicated to advancing his career in the medical profession, but he was also short, unattractive and not especially attentive to the needs of a young wife. She soon got bored and embarked on numerous affairs, culminating in one particularly reckless and public liaison with a married viscount.

The papers were full of gossip about her indiscreet behaviour, and in 1774 her husband applied to the ecclesiastical courts for a legal separation. Her family were highly embarrassed at her conduct and packed her off to a French convent to reflect on her wicked ways, but almost immediately she was 'rescued' by Lord Cholmondeley. He provided her with 'high keeping' and for a number of years she was his mistress, although this was not an exclusive arrangement for either party. She was given the nickname 'Dally the Tall' and made for an improbable sight when she went out on the town with her friend, the diminutive Gertrude Mahon.

The pair were seen arm in arm with Lord Cholmondeley when they visited the Pantheon for a Ball in 1776, and the gossip-mongers were keen to conjecture that he was simultaneously enjoying bedroom delights with both companions, long and short.

In her case, Grace had affairs with the Prince of Wales, and with various members of the aristocracy. In 1784 she ended up as the mistress of the Duc d'Orleans and moved to France to be with him. Come the Revolution and it appears that she and her lover were on opposite sides: he supported the revolutionaries and abandoned his title; she was staunchly royalist and a firm friend of Madame du Barry, the official mistress of Louis XV. In the Reign of Terror all her royal friends lost their heads. She narrowly escaped the same fate, and instead languished in a series of French prisons until her release in 1794. She stayed on in France, and later was rumoured to have had an affair with Napoleon Bonaparte. He is alleged to have proposed marriage to her, but she declined. Her memoirs entitled the *Journal of my life during the French Revolution* were published by her grand-daughter in 1859, and although some of the events recounted are inaccurate, or are composites of actual events, they do reveal a brave and fascinating woman, who lived life on her own terms.

Mary 'Perdita' Robinson 1757–1800

The daughter of a Bristol-based naval captain who abandoned her mother and four siblings, Mary had an inauspicious start to life. At sixteen she was already married, a mother of a young child, and the whole family had been imprisoned for debt. She secured an acting role, where her good looks quickly attracted the attention of the young Prince of Wales. The prince offered her a bond in the sum of £20,000 as a sort of signing-on fee, payable when she was twenty-one, if she would become his mistress. She agreed, and for several months enjoyed spending extravagantly on clothes, jewellery and so on.

She was given the nickname of 'Perdita' after the part she played on stage and for which she was famous: Perdita in Shakespeare's *A Midsummer Night's Dream*. The Prince happily used the *nom de plume* Florizel, who in the play falls in love with Perdita. The affair was conducted under a very public spotlight, with almost daily updates appearing in newspapers. So, in June 1781, readers of the *Morning Herald* were informed that: 'Fortune has again smiled on Perdita; on Sunday she sported an entire new phaeton, drawn by four chestnut-coloured ponies, with a postillion and servant in blue and silver liveries. The lady dashed into town through Hyde Park turnpike at four o'clock, dressed in a blue great-coat prettily trimmed in silver; a plume of feathers graced her hat, which even Alexander the Great might have prided himself in.'

After the prince dumped her barely a year into the relationship – and tried to renege on paying her the money due under the bond – she had a succession of wealthy lovers, including the politician Charles James Fox, Lord Malden and, later, the dashing soldier Banastre Tarleton. She fell deeply in love with Tarleton and lived with him on and off for fifteen years, going on to become the pre-eminent fashionista of her generation. Newspapers dined out on stories of every new lover, with the *Morning Post* of 21 September 1782 breathlessly reporting that:

> Yesterday, a messenger arrived in town, with the very interesting and pleasing intelligence of the Tarleton, armed ship, having, after a chace of some months, captured the Perdita frigate, and brought her safe into Egham port. The Perdita is a prodigious fine clean bottomed vessel, and had taken many prizes during her cruize, particularly the Florizel, a most valuable ship belonging to the Crown, but which was immediately released, after taking out the cargo. The Perdita was captured some time ago by the Fox, but was, afterwards, retaken by the Malden, and had a sumptuous suit of new rigging, when she fell in with the Tarleton. Her manoeuvering to escape was admirable; but the Tarleton, fully determined to take her, or perish, would not give up the chace; and at length, coming alongside the Perdita, fully determined to board her, sword in hand, she instantly surrendered at discretion.

She went to Paris, and on her return created a sensation by turning up at the opera wearing the latest that French fashion had to offer. Hats, gowns and so on were all named after her. And where she went, and what she wore, was faithfully reported. In 1784 the *Morning Post* and *Daily Advertiser* of Saturday, 25 September reported with a nudge and a wink that: 'It is not true, that the Perdita is gone into a Convent of Nuns in France; she is indeed retired, but not amongst the female part of the religious; certain friars, it is said, have found her a very warm convert!'

However, the *Rambler's Magazine* of much the same time reported that:

'Mrs Robinson has been lately obliged to leave England, for the continent, for the recovery of her health. She has almost lost the use of her limbs, and, upon her journey, was lifted in and out of her carriage. Her disorder is a rheumatic gout of so obstinate a nature that her recovery is doubtful.'

When Tarleton deserted her, she wrote sad and moving poems about their doomed relationship. In 1783 she had suffered a miscarriage, which left her partially paralysed, and she spent the last fifteen years of her life in declining health. She started to write her autobiography, but died at the age of forty-three on Boxing Day 1800, and the biography was completed by her daughter. History now recognizes her as a fine writer and an early campaigner for the rights of women, but in her lifetime she was more famous for her lovers and for her innate fashion sense.

Frances Abington 1737–1815

Born Frances Barton to a father who was either a mercenary soldier, or a cobbler, Frances was put to work selling flowers in the streets near Covent Garden, earning her the name 'Nosegay Fan'. By her early teens she was using her fine singing voice as a street singer, and then became a child prostitute. By 1773 she had her own listing in *Harris's List of Covent Garden Ladies*. She later came to the attention of the actor/theatre manager David Garrick, who had a soft spot for the elfin-like chanteuse. He gave her a job at the Drury Lane Theatre, where she quickly became famous for her comedic roles especially as Miss Prue, in the play *Love For Love*.

She had her portrait painted on at least half a dozen occasions by Sir Joshua Reynolds, who appears to have had a particularly emotional bond with his muse.

At the height of her fame she was renowned for her dress style and sense of fashion. Then, as now, if an outfit was seen on a fashion icon, it appeared in shops in the High Street a matter of a few days later. The theatre companies pandered to this fame, since people would come to the theatre just to see what she was wearing, and gave her a dress allowance accordingly, i.e. a payment of £500 per annum, over and above her salary as an actress.

After each performance young rakes with deep pockets would queue up to secure her favours for the rest of the evening. It was an era where most actresses were available for hire at the end of a performance, and when 'actress' was often a pseudonym for 'whore'. She finally retired at the age of sixty and spent her last seventeen years in comparative wealth, courtesy of an inheritance from a wealthy admirer.

Elizabeth Armistead 1750–1842

Of all the courtesans of the eighteenth century, Elizabeth Armistead was perhaps the most remarkable. Remarkable for the extent of her glittering clientele, for living to the age of ninety-one, and for finding true love with one of the most charismatic and rakish politicians of the period.

She did not have an easy start in life. By the time she was nineteen she was working in a high-class brothel. This energetic young lady with a warm personality and an impressive physique was extremely popular, and she was soon in high keeping thanks to a large number of ardent followers. It was said that she could 'claim the conquest of two ducal coronets, a marquis, four earls and a viscount'.

Certainly, her client list included the Prince of Wales, the Duke of Dorset, the Duke of Ancaster, the Earl of Derby, Viscount Bolingbroke, Lord George Cavendish and the fabulously wealthy General Sir Richard Smith. The Earl of Cholmondeley, Lord Robert Spencer and Lord Coleraine were also benefactors. Through her talents she acquired enough wealth to buy herself at least two properties, in Bond Street and in Clarges Street, in Mayfair, and quickly became known as 'the Toast of the Town'.

She was pre-eminent in her field for an astonishing ten years during which time she was a fashion icon, a centre of gossip, and an inspiration to many. The press revelled in the fact that she succeeded Perdita (Mary Robinson) as the prince's mistress, with the *Morning Herald* of 8 February 1781 commenting that: 'Mrs. Arm…..d has certainly been gratified at last in an amour with a certain young personage; and now flatters herself that her charms will not be so soon unrivetted, as were those of the once exalted and enviable Perdita.'

In 1783 she fell for the charms of Charles James Fox, the Whig politician renowned for his six o-clock stubble, his gambling addiction, his womanising and his drinking. Theirs was a love-match which astonished society, a case of Beauty and the Beast. But love it was, and it stood the test of time, as well as derision from some quarters, and a lack of acceptance into 'polite society'. The depth of Fox's feelings was shown in one of his many letters to Elizabeth, where he writes: 'You shall not go without me, wherever you go. I have examined myself and know that I can better abandon friends, country, everything than live without Liz. I could change my name and live with you in the remotest part of Europe in poverty and obscurity. I could bear that very well, but to be parted I cannot bear.'

For her part, Elizabeth even sold her properties to pay off Fox's gambling debts, set up home with him at St Anne's in Surrey, and introduced him to the delights of gardening and country living. For ten years they lived discreetly as mistress and keeper, with Elizabeth resisting suggestions that they marry because of the scandal that it might cause. She eventually gave in to his entreaties, on condition that the union was kept under wraps, and they married in secret in 1795.

It was not until 1802, when the couple embarked for Paris to meet the Emperor Napoleon, that Fox decided to go public. There was a brief period of gossip and tut-tutting, but the fuss quickly died down, largely thanks to Elizabeth's charm, good nature and tolerance. Fox died in 1806, leaving her to carry on as a lonely widow for thirty-five years. Respect for her was enormous: she was awarded a pension of £1,200 per annum, and in 1823 her former lover, now King George IV, gave her an annuity of £500.

That annuity was continued by the King's brother, William IV, when he succeeded to the throne, and indeed by Victoria when she became Queen in 1837. Throughout those years she was untouched by scandal, never once attempted to 'kiss and tell', and died beloved by the local community.

Harriette Dubouchet aka Harriette Wilson 1786–1845

Harriette was perhaps the best-known courtesan of the Regency era. She was one of five sisters who reached maturity. One, and only one of the five, chose not to become a sex worker. She was dubbed 'The Paragon'. The other four made their mark as courtesans, but none scaled the heights of her profession as successfully as Harriette. She was considered a late starter, becoming mistress to the Earl of Craven at fifteen. Other wealthy patrons followed, and she ended up with an impressive list of clients, which included the Prince of Wales, the Lord Chancellor and four future prime ministers.

When she was thirty-five years old, Harriette astonished everyone by retiring from harlotry. She got married to a man called Rochfort, hopped on a boat to France, and then decided that it was pay-back time. She published her memoirs one instalment at a time, ending each one with a list of the famous names to be included in the following instalment (unless the persons named paid up). Yes, it was blackmail, but it was a very open and straightforward form of blackmail. Her targets were principally men who had promised her money in her retirement, or an annuity, but had gone back on their word. The strategy used by Harriette was extremely effective, and the public were enthralled with her under-the-bedclothes revelations.

Harriette supposedly made £10,000 out of the venture. One of the men she tried to get money out of was the Duke of Wellington. He declined to be blackmailed, though whether or not he used the phrase 'Publish and be damned' is far from certain. Denied any money, she duly published, and informed the world that Wellington had no small-talk and described him as looking like a rat-catcher.

Her book, entitled *The Memoirs of Harriette Wilson, Written by Herself*, first published in 1825, is still in print. It is celebrated for its opening line: 'I shall not say how and why I became, at the age of fifteen, the mistress of the Earl of Craven'. As a kiss-and-tell book it is a spirited attack on the leaders of society who had been happy to promise her annuities, wealth, respectability and support, only to go back on their words when it suited them.

* * *

So, what are we to make of this snap-shot of some of the stars who made it to the top of the tree? Looking at their portraits, many of them painted by the leading artists of the day, they may not appear beautiful to modern eyes, but in the eighteenth century they defined beauty, taste, fashion and style. In many cases they seem to have been shared around by the same small circle of princes and aristocrats. Many of them died young, but a few of them enjoyed a lifestyle unattainable by any other form of employment.

They really did know how to succeed in a man's world. Newspapers reported on their every public appearance, describing what they were wearing and how they styled their hair. They may not have been made welcome in the salons and dining rooms of the grand homes built by their aristocratic lovers, but on their own turf, in their own demi-monde, they reigned supreme. No attempt was made to disguise the fact that they earned their money through the sale of sexual favours, and in an age before super-injunctions and Press Council restraint, the public knew exactly who was doing what with whom.

Nancy Parsons and the Third Duke of Grafton, from the *Town & Country Magazine*.

Chapter 5

Of Virginity and Masturbation, of Dildos and Sex Aids

Virginity

It has been suggested that at the start of the eighteenth century less than one per cent of all births were calculated to have taken place outside marriage, yet by 1800 it is estimated that twenty per cent of all children were born out of wedlock. Clearly, that would suggest a significant change in the amount of pre-marital sex taking place, and also a slightly more relaxed attitude towards illegitimacy. However, any such relaxation of the way bastardy was looked at was confined to the lower orders; the non property-owning section of the great British public. For the land-owning classes, for the aristocracy concerned about their hereditary estates and titles, legitimacy was everything: an illegitimate child did not and could not inherit from its parents.

Dildos, dildos, who'll buy my dildo?

But if sex before marriage was less frowned upon, that did not mean that there was any less emphasis on the value of a girl's virginity. If anything, the rarer it became the more value was placed upon it!

The Church has always put great store by virginity: not just in the narrowest sense of a girl who had never had sex, but in its wider meaning of a woman, single or married, who led a chaste, virginal life. The Catholic Church, in particular, was happy for a married couple to engage in sex if it was done with a view to procreate. But take away the intention of having a family, and the belief was that you should show piety by abstaining from sex; that you should show solidarity with the saints being worshipped by fasting and abstaining from sex. Being chaste was a sign of devotion, and this was at a time when the calendar was crammed full with Saints Days. Nowadays we are lucky if we remember the four patron saints of Great Britain, but even in the Anglican Church the calendar of Common Worship generally lists around twenty days in every calendar month which are dedicated to remembering one saint or another.

For the Roman Catholic Church the number of occasions when chastity could be called for was endless: the saints are listed in a 776-page volume entitled *Roman Martyrology*, and even that is not an exhaustive compilation of all the saints venerated in the Catholic Church. While Catholicism was largely driven underground in the eighteenth century its tradition of abstinence on Saints Days remained strong, and was probably a very significant reason why more women did not spend their entire adult lives getting pregnant. 'Not tonight dear, I've got a Saints Day,' must have been a common example of chastity in a God-fearing population. The individual saints and their days were marked in red in the diaries and almanacs: they were, literally, red letter days.

Taken as a whole, the vast majority of the British population in the first half of the eighteenth century were members of the Anglican Church: well over ninety per cent. However, that Church lost nearly one fifth of its market share during the 'long' eighteenth century; in other words, up to the end of the Georgian era. Inevitably, the tradition of abstinence became less widespread during this period, as the tentacles of religious control started to relax.

When John Wesley founded the Methodist movement he was of the view that studying the lives of famous saints was important, but that worshipping them was meaningless, saying that 'most of the holy days were at present answering no valuable end'. Article XIV of the Articles of Religion of the Methodist Church went further, stating: 'The Romish doctrine concerning [...] worshiping, and adoration, as well of images as of relics, and also invocation of saints, is a fond thing, vainly invented, and grounded upon no warrant of Scripture, but repugnant to the Word of God.'

The Baptists, another important group classified as Dissenters, did not recognize canonized saints in the same way as the Catholic and Anglican Churches, but they were still often seen as important Christian leaders and theologians. The Quakers went a stage further, and historically did not regard even Christmas Day and Easter Day as being any different to any other days of the year. Christ's birth and resurrection were to be remembered throughout the year. So no saints day ban on sex for them, simply a belief that sins are actions that involve the exploitation of another person and that chastity is the total absence of such exploitation. But for the vast majority of the population, there was a general feeling that saints should be venerated, that veneration involved chastity, and that this was a jolly good way of controlling unwanted pregnancies.

Virginity in its strict medical sense – the condition of a woman who has not had sex, as opposed to the ecclesiastical view of a woman who chooses to follow a path of chastity – was still seen as being of great importance, and of significant financial value. Marrying a virgin was one way of ensuring paternity: at least the first-born child of that marriage could be expected to be a legitimate offspring, entitled to inherit wealth and status.

This 'value' of virginity was reflected in the literature of the time. Back in the 1670s Aphra Behn had written a short story called *The Unfortunate Happy Lady: A True History*. It tells the tale of an innocent girl sold to a brothel by her dissolute brother. A rake pays for her virginity but then falls in love with her instead, and she with him. When they first meet the rake says to his intended 'victim': 'Don't you know then that you are in a naughty house and that old Beldam is a rank procuress to whom I am to give 200 guineas for your Maidenhead?' Two hundred guineas was a huge sum. Even a century later an agricultural worker would be expected to work for ten years to earn that sort of money.

The value of virginity in the marketplace is nowhere more apparent than in John Clelands's *Memoirs of a Woman of Pleasure*. Probably no other book in English literature prior to this had ever been so graphic, with its description of Fanny Hill losing her virginity to her lover. On an earlier occasion Fanny had outwitted a lecherous 'liquorish old goat' who had paid Mother Brown for the privilege of deflowering her. In Fanny's words: 'Mrs Brown had in the meantime agreed terms [...] which I afterwards understood were to be fifty guineas peremptory for the liberty of attempting me and a hundred more at the complete gratification of his desires, in the triumph over my virginity.' Fifty pounds down as a reservation fee and another hundred on completion made virginity, real or otherwise, a valuable commodity. As it happened the 'old goat' suffered from premature ejaculation, leaving Fanny *virgo intacta*.

Literature also makes it clear that feminine wiles meant that a woman could easily pretend virginity in order to secure a high price for her virtue. In *Shamela*, a satirical spoof of Samuel Richardson's *Pamela – or Virtue Rewarded*, Henry Fielding makes Shamela confess on her wedding night: 'I behaved with as much Bashfulness as the purest Virgin in the World could ever have done. The most difficult task for me was to blush; however, by holding my breath and squeezing my cheeks with my handkerchief I did pretty well.'

From a male point of view, the presence of blood was considered the surest way of indicating that the hymen had been broken, and therefore it became the main way that a woman who was no longer a virgin could persuade her eager lover of her purity. It was comparatively easy to conceal a phial of chicken blood under the bed clothes, to smear on the sheets at the appropriate time. Other devices included the insertion of a small piece of sponge, soaked in lamb's blood, into the vagina. One good thrust from the man and Hey Presto!, a touch of blood would mark the occasion. That still left the question of how to pull the wool over the eyes of a man who expected to feel resistance, but even that could be faked. For centuries it had been believed that a ruptured hymen could be mended by administering a vaginal fumigant made from burning herbs. That was, of course, nonsense, but perhaps more likely to confuse the hapless male was the use of a resin suppository, giving the impression of resistance during penetration.

Men also gave great credence to tightly furled lips of labia, thinking that they were a sign of virginity, and believing that past sexual activity would be evidenced by what was coyly described as *souillure clitoriedienne*, an elongated clitoris. So, brothel keepers wanting to 'sell' the virginity of their girls over and over again would attempt to fool male customers by 'shrivelling' the labial lips. How? There were a number of recommended ways, the main one being the use of an astringent such as alum water. Grose's Dictionary even had a name for it, pucker water, which was defined as, 'water impregnated with alum, or other astringents, used by old experienced traders to counterfeit virginity'. Alum water was actually a compound of hydrated potassium and aluminium sulphate and the fact that it was in general use is reflected in the works of numerous writers of the time. It had been known for its astringent qualities since the days of Ancient Greece, and was in widespread use throughout the Georgian era. Small wonder, when a 'pre-used' sex worker might be able to charge only a few guineas for her services, whereas a 're-virginised' girl could command perhaps fifty times that amount. Other madams may have recommended 'restoring maidenhead' by taking a bath in comfrey roots (following a recommendation in the 1684 book entitled *Aristotle's Masterpiece*).

In this way Fanny Hill is able to sell her 'pretended virginity' to Mr Norbert, a man with a predilection for deflowering young virgins and abandoning them afterwards. For a fee of 300 guineas (and another 100 paid to a broker) Fanny is introduced to Mr Norbert while 'breathing nothing but that innocence which the men so ardently require in us, for no other end than to feast themselves with the pleasure of destroying it.' She declines to use alum water ('I had no occasion to borrow those auxiliaries of art that create a momentary one, easily discovered by the test of a warm bath'), but instead deceives her purchaser by using a blood-soaked sponge: 'In each of the head bed-posts, just above where the bedsteads are inserted into them, there was a small drawer, so artfully adapted to the mouldings of the timber-work, that it might have escaped even the most curious search: which drawers were easily opened or shut by the touch of a spring, and were fitted each with a shallow glass tumbler, full of a prepared fluid blood, in which lay soaked, for ready use, a sponge.'

Men could always be found who wanted to be 'the first'. For them it was the Holy Grail, boldly going where no man had gone before. And judging by the stories of modern-day students auctioning off their virginity on the internet for thousands of pounds, the lure of what the historian Edmund Gibbons described as being 'the glorious crown of virginity' has never gone away.

There was one particular reason why men would pay more for the privilege of deflowering: virgins would not be infectious with venereal disease. It was not only considered safer to have sex with a virgin: in a cruelly twisted logic it was thought that if an infected man had sex with a virgin her 'purity' would in itself drive out the disease. It finds an echo in modern cases where men infected by HIV deliberately choose to have unprotected sex with a healthy partner, in a mistaken belief that this can bring about a cure.

Masturbation

In one area more than any other, medical opinion echoed the teachings of religious leaders: masturbation was bad. Known in the eighteenth century as onanism, masturbation led to an imbalance of humours. In an era where men allowed themselves to believe that penetration was the be-all and end-all, and that this was all that was needed to bring a woman to climax, the idea of masturbation, mutual or otherwise, seemed wasteful. For a woman it showed a shocking venality, a taste of the forbidden fruit which had led Eve to her downfall. For a man it was debilitating. And, of course, the Bishop of London knew that it caused earthquakes.

Discussion in medical circles really got going after 1715 with the publication of *Onania*, a pamphlet that warned of 'stunted growth, disorders of the penis and testes, gonorrhoea, epilepsy, hysteria, consumption, and barrenness.' A more considered analysis, involving cod-science and purported case studies, was a book by Samuel Auguste Tissot published in 1763 entitled *L' Onanisme*. It was swiftly translated into English and published as *Onanism*, becoming the definitive study of 'self pollution'.

Tissot quotes Hippocrates, who described masturbation as the cause of an illness given the name of dorsal consumption: 'This disease arises from the dorsal portion of the spinal marrow. It principally attacks young married people or the licentious […] They have a sensation of ants crawling from the head down along the spine […] They lose the powers of procreation, yet often dream of venereal pleasures. They become very weak, and walking produces shortness of breath; they have pains in the head and ringing in the ears; finally, an acute fever supervenes and then they die.'

Tissot emphasised the link between the eyes and the testicles, writing: 'I have myself known a man fifty-nine years of age, who, three weeks after marrying a young wife, became blind and in four months died.' Tissot identified seminal fluids with animal spirits, and the loss of either had severe consequences. He quotes one authority as saying: 'After long nocturnal pollutions the patient not only loses strength, becomes emaciated and pale, and the memory is impaired; a continual sensation of coldness affects all the extremities, the sight becomes dim, the voice harsh, and the whole body is gradually wasted. Sleep is disturbed by unpleasant dreams, does not refresh, and pains are like those produced by bruises.'

In his opinion 'young people of both sexes who indulge in lasciviousness ruin their health by wasting strength which was designed to make them vigorous, and finally fall into consumption.' He also identifies diarrhoea, pimples on the face, sterility, memory loss, stomach ache and epilepsy as being attributable to masturbation. In women, onanism led to 'attacks of hysteria, melancholy, incurable jaundice, acute pains in the stomach and back, *fluor albus*, *prolapsus* and ulceration of the uterus and their consequences, as well as elongation of the clitoris … which deprives them of both modesty and reason and places them on a level with the most lascivious brutes until death terminates their career.'

There was a particular problem with girls masturbating before their bodies were full-grown: it could lead to girls becoming thin and emaciated, growth would be irregular and, in some cases, halted. This was thought to lead to curvature of the spine. Even more terrible, it produced in females 'an indifference to the lawful pleasures of marriage'. Tissot particularly mentions a case he was involved with where the vice 'has produced such an effect on the senses of the woman that she has no inclination for lawful intercourse.'

What comes across is a medical profession which had not moved forward since the days of the Roman Empire. Good old Galen was dusted off and his four humours were used to justify the attack on masturbation:

a wasted ejection of seminal fluid was creating an imbalance, and this was at a time when the fluid, whether male or female, was considered to be just as important to human life as blood itself. Also, masturbation was harmful because it caused loss of vital humours in the form of perspiration. With ordinary intercourse, healthy humours are exchanged between the two parties involved. But a solo masturbator would lose vital fluids without receiving anything in return. Doctors needed to look no further than the inmates of asylums such as Bedlam. Why, these mental deficients masturbated, a sure sign of the link between onanism and insanity.

Not all medical advice was opposed to masturbatory stimulation. Some even recommended it, under medical control, as a cure for hysteria. As already mentioned, this was seen as a disease affecting women who were deprived of a normal sex life. In such cases the doctor might decide that it was wise to administer manual stimulation. It was a time when hysteria was referred to as 'the widow's disease', and doctors believed that a female produced her own form of semen. It was thought to become poisonous if not released through regular climax or intercourse.

Half a century earlier Pieter van Foreest, published a medical compendium titled *Observationem et Curationem Medicinalium ac Chirurgicarum Opera Omnia*. It contained a chapter on female ailments and in 1653 offered this advice: 'When these symptoms indicate, we think it necessary to ask a midwife to assist, so that she can massage the genitalia with one finger inside, using oil of lilies, musk root, crocus, or [something] similar. And in this way the afflicted woman can be aroused to the paroxysm. This kind of stimulation with the finger is recommended by Galen and Avicenna, among others, most especially for widows, those who live chaste lives, and religious females.'

The drawback is that this treatment took up a lot of the good doctor's time, which no doubt could be put to better use, well, more profitable use, treating other patients. In the previous century the English surgeon Nathaniel Highmore, who died in 1685, had commented that the treatment was not always straightforward, writing that it was similar to 'that game of boys in which they try to rub their stomachs with one hand and pat their heads with the other'.

A doctor could hardly delegate the task of manual stimulation to an unqualified helper, and although the first mechanical vibrator was probably not invented until the following century, there are reports that a Frenchman invented a clockwork massager called a *tremoussoir* in 1734. What is more probable is that doctors discovered that a jet of warm water could offer 'relief'; the orgasm was known as hysterical paroxysm. When Tobias Smollett, a Scottish doctor who later became a playwright and author, visited Bath in 1752 he noted, without explanation, that the spa had a number of female devices offering 'hydriatic massage'. At the same time, he noted in his 'Essay on the External Use of Water' that the mineral waters of Bath had little advantage, if any, over any other water. Whatever water was used, hydriatic massage gained in popularity throughout the eighteenth century, with the introduction of electric vibrators not appearing until the mid-1880s.

For women wanting to pleasure themselves there were dildos available; maybe not on open display on shop counters, as suggested by the image at the start of this chapter, but still made commercially. These had been around for centuries, were often made out of leather stuffed with fabric or animal hair, and would either be available from specialist shops (Mrs Phillips in Covent Garden's Half Moon Street, under the sign of the Green Canister, is usually cited) or perhaps from enterprising cordwainers (shoe makers) who would stitch these handy 'consolateurs' or 'widow's comforters' out of stiffened leather. A quick application of olive oil and the dildo would be ready to use. Other dildos, designed for wealthier ladies, might be made of ebony and, more often, ivory. Some surviving examples reveal that some of these were hollow and equipped with a plunger, to enable liquid, such as milk, to be ejected at the critical moment in simulation of a male ejaculation.

Perhaps unsurprisingly, such devices rarely feature in eighteenth-century art or literature, but there are fascinating glimpses in some of the trials mentioned in the Newgate Calendar. One involved Mary Hamilton, aka George Hamilton, who dressed as a Methodist preacher and exchanged marriage vows with a wealthy widow by the name of Mrs Rushford. 'George' managed to deceive his bride by using a dildo. The extraordinary story was subsequently told by the writer Henry Fielding in a pamphlet called *The Female Husband*, although Fielding declines to mention the word 'dildo' and instead prefers to describe the deception by means 'which decency forbids me even to mention.' More about this and other remarkable same-sex 'marriages' appears in Chapter 13.

Of Virginity and Masturbation, of Dildos and Sex Aids   61

Still on the subject of masturbation, there were also clubs, for males only, where sex acts would be performed on a collective basis. The best known of these was the Beggar's Benison, based in the town of Anstruther on the Firth of Forth, but apparently with another club intended for Manchester, if contemporary newspaper reports are to be believed. At first sight these clubs appear to be homoerotic gatherings, where men would 'knock penises' before ejaculating into a special bowl. In fact, this appears to have been more akin to an initiation ceremony, embellished with procedures not unlike some of the rituals followed by the Freemasons. Prior to the mutual ejaculation one or more 'posture molls' would be introduced to the male audience (females who would strip off to show their genitalia in a scene recorded by Thomas Rowlandson in his sketch entitled *Cunnyseurs*, shown at page 163). Other clubs, such as the notorious Hellfire Club (originally known as the Brotherhood of St Francis of Wycombe) met at Medmenham Abbey. Here, harlots such as the young Fanny Murray would parade before eager members, while dressed (or rather, undressed) as nuns. There were in fact a number of other clubs which went by the name of 'hellfire' and all had the same connection with organised orgies, open to club members who shared their sexual experiences.

The Beggar's Benison Test Platter.

Chapter 6

Aphrodisiacs, Libido and Fertility

In 1684 a book appeared in print under one of the most fancifully false titles ever, *Aristotle's Masterpiece*. It had nothing whatsoever to do with Aristotle and it was no masterpiece. It was merely a 'cut and paste' job by an anonymous writer, merging earlier texts on midwifery and the marvels of the natural world. But it became a long-running best seller, with dozens and dozens of reprints lasting well into the nineteenth century. In the 1700s it marked the start of a move away from the teachings of Galen, and incorporated prevailing ideas on natural medicines, herbs and what we would now call holistic medicine. If a Georgian woman was unable to conceive and wanted to know what to do about it, all she had to do was consult her edition of the *Masterpiece*. There it was, in black and white:

The root of the mandrake – a sure-fire cure for poor performance.

> If barrenness proceeds from overmuch heat, let her use inwardly, succory, endive, violets, water-lillies, sorrel and lettuce, with syrups and conserves made thus: take conserve of borage, violets, succory, water-lillies, of each an ounce; half an ounce of conserve of roses […] with syrup of violets, or juice of citron, make an electuary. Let her also take of endive, water-lillies, and borage flowers of each a handful; rhubarb, myrobolans of each three drams; with water make

a decoction; add to the straining, the syrup laxative of violets one ounce, syrup of cassia half an ounce, manna three drams; make all into a potion. Take of the syrup of mugwort one ounce, syrup of maidenhair two ounces, pulv.elect.trionsat. make all up into a julep. Apply to the veins and privities fomentations of the juice of lettuce violets, roses, mallows, vine leaves and nightshade: let her also anoint her secret parts with the cooling ointment of galls.

The same book advised the young lady to have plenty of baths, breathe fresh air, wear light clothes and eat plenty of lettuce and endives. She was to avoid strong alcohol and instead drink watered-down wine. She was to take plenty of rest, could sleep as much as she wanted but 'must use but little copulation'.

Other writers regarded infertility as a purely female problem, considering it the woman's fault if conception did not happen. Quack doctors were always on hand to promote pills and potions, with one newspaper advertisement from 'a Doctor of Physick' claiming that he could cure, 'Fits of the Mother, Vapours rising up to the Throat, Passions or Tremblings of the Heart, Obstructions, Convulsions, Green Sickness, Weakness and Pains of the Back.' The good doctor could also 'make fruitful, take away the cause of Barrenness or impotence in Men or Women, which secret preserves youth and prolongs life.'

Quack remedies got over the embarrassment of a woman having to be examined by a male doctor. With a nostrum offered for sale in the newspapers, the woman could see for herself the range of infirmities cured by the proffered remedy. She could make her purchase, anonymously, and administer the cure in private. And, of course, many of the advertisements offered money-back guarantees, or in some cases offered to forgo all payments until conception took place.

The eighteenth century also saw some genuine medical advances in the treatment of sexual problems. In the early 1770s a Scottish doctor by the name of John Hunter advised a cloth merchant with severe hypospadias (i.e. a deformed or faulty penis) to collect his semen in a warmed syringe and to inject it into his wife's vagina. Hunter has been described as 'the founder of scientific surgery', and was certainly the father of what might now be crudely termed 'the turkey-basting technique'. In this case it worked, but the technique was not always successful, largely because it took another 100 years for the medical profession to work out exactly when ovulation occurred, with some believing that conception could only take place during menstruation.

Dr Hunter was an enigmatic but brilliant doctor and in 1776 he was appointed as royal physician to King George III. He appears to have had a penchant for self-experimentation. Unfortunately, this proved unwise, especially when he decided to use himself as a guinea-pig for the treatment of syphilis and gonorrhoea. However, in 1786 these researches led him to publish *A Treatise on the Venereal Diseases*, one of the first texts to discuss venereal disease in a non-judgmental manner, and in turn led to further research into the causes and treatment of infertility and impotence.

So much for combating the dreadful condition of being barren; there was still the problem of getting in the mood for love. *Aristotle's Masterpiece* contained the answer, prescribing: 'Hen-Eggs, Pheasants, Woodcocks, Gnatsappers, Thrushes, Black Birds, young Pigeons, Sparrows, Partridge, Capons, Almonds, Pine-Nuts, Raysons, Currants, all strong Wines moderately taken; especially those made of the Grapes of Italy.' For men, it advised that, 'Erection is chiefly caused and provoked by Satyrium Eringoes, Cresses, Erysimum, Parsnips, Artichoaks, Turnips, Rapes, Asparagus, Candid Ginger, Gallinga, Acorns bruised to Powder, and drank in Muscadel, Scallions, Sea Shell-Fish, &c.'

The same book informed readers that if the woman wanted to produce a boy she should lie on her right side after copulation, and for good measure should increase the chances of a male child by knocking back 'Spirit of Saffron and juice of Hyssop [i.e. mint].'

The unknown author of *Aristotle's Masterpiece* with his cobbled-together herbal remedies was following a path laid down by the herbalist Nicholas Culpeper who, in 1652, brought out *The English Physician* (later renamed *The Complete Herbal*). Many editions followed in the ensuing century, and it was still going strong 150 years later. In particular, the late Georgian era saw editions appearing in 1798, 1805 and 1813. The book satisfied the desire of the gardening public to learn about the medicinal properties of many of the new plant varieties brought into Britain by the great plantsmen of the Elizabethan and Stuart periods.

Herbs from the New World, added to the native collection of plants, provided a rich source of aphrodisiacs. Galium, commonly known as 'bedstraw', would increase libido in both men and women if it was boiled in oil and then eaten, or applied externally as a stimulant. Culpeper was also a great advocate of the powers of asparagus, writing that it 'stirreth up bodily lust in man and woman' alike. The French certainly took this to heart and often served several courses of asparagus at wedding feasts.

Other aphrodisiacs owed their popularity to their appearance: avocado pears were regarded as representing the testicles of the male because of the way they hung in pairs from the branches of the tree; peaches were popular because their rounded shape resembled a pair of buttocks. Fruit with lots of seeds – figs and pomegranates for instance – were regarded as 'sexy foods' because they were compared to the seeds of fertility. Throughout the eighteenth century more and more plants and animals were added to the list, with phallically shaped carrots becoming popular. And who could doubt the mystic powers of the mandrake root, particularly if it were shaped like the one shown at the start of this chapter.

Onions and other vegetable bulbs considered to resemble testicles were much favoured, while both eels and oysters were popular because they resembled, respectively, the male and female sex organs. Oysters probably had their biggest boost in popularity when Casanova was reported to get through fifty a day, and the humble bi-valve has never looked back.

Another writer recommended boiling ants in oil, writing that the '*Oleum Formicarum*,' when applied to the genitals, 'is reported to occasion venereal Erections, beyond all those Remedies directed inwardly, whether Perfumes, Aromaticks, Analepticks or others, prescrib'd as Aphrodisiacks.' Somehow you get the impression that by the time the man has gone out to catch a cupful of ants, boiled them in oil, allowed them to cool (presumably) and then rubbed them gently into his manhood, his lady might well have lost all interest, blown out the candle, or settled down to a good read of *Paradise Lost*.

Rather more mainstream was the idea that another insect was good for arousing the dormant male member: Spanish fly (otherwise known as cantharides). Spanish fly was obtained from a beetle (*Lytta vesicatoria*) found in countries adjoining the Mediterranean. One side-effect of its continued use was that it could irritate the urinary tract resulting in priapism, an abnormally prolonged erection caused by the dilation of blood vessels in the penis. It could also cause vomiting and diarrhoea, and, ironically, lead to erectile dysfunction. Not that that put off the Marquis de Sade, who reportedly gave aniseed-flavoured pastilles laced with Spanish fly to two prostitutes in 1772. They were both poisoned and very nearly died. At a subsequent trial, the marquis was given the death sentence after he was found guilty of attempting to kill them, and also for the crime of sodomy. He appealed against the sentence and was eventually reprieved.

Nowadays, science tells us that there is no proof that any particular food has any effect on libido – it is all in the mind – but, in general, foods which are smooth, rich, creamy exotic or spicy – or which resemble sex organs – have always been popular. Anise, mustard, nettles, and sweet peas were commonly considered aphrodisiacs, along with peppers. Galen had taught that flatulums – vegetables that produced wind – were performance-enhancing, which is slightly contrary to what we might expect, but arose from the belief that having wind would help inflate the penis. It is hard to imagine that there were many adherents to Galen's ideas or that a Galen cookery book would ever be a bestseller.

So far as liquids were concerned, both coffee and chocolate were incredibly popular in the eighteenth century, having been introduced into England during the middle of the previous century. Consumption moved from the coffee houses into the homes of those aspiring to be respectable and rich, and active between the sheets. Both concoctions satisfied the test of being hot and moist, and both were admired for their arousing qualities. Tea-drinking was also regarded as being beneficial: in 1773 Dr Thomas Percival made an extensive investigation into the population statistics of Manchester and its surrounding areas. He estimated that each marriage resulted in around four and three-quarter children, and, unlike most of his contemporaries, decided that this was evidence of an increase in the population. He concluded that fertility had been promoted by the general use of tea, or possibly pepper and other spices: you could take your pick.

And then of course there was alcohol: known by Shakespeare for its ability to 'provoke the desire, but also take away the performance' (*Macbeth*). The eighteenth century was a time of excessive alcohol consumption across the social spectrum, from the gin craze destroying the poor – and so sharply observed by William Hogarth – to the befuddled aristocrat drunk on imported brandy or port wine. Alcohol may have inflamed the passions, but can hardly have been regarded as an effective performance-booster.

Moving on from food and drink, treatment of all manner of sexual ailments was dealt with at the newly fashionable spas which sprang up all over the country. Looking just at the area west of London, the spring at Leamington Spa had been known since Roman times but was rediscovered in 1784. In Clifton, Bristol, the spring at Hotwells was leased to the Society of Merchant Venturers in 1692, enabling them to build pump rooms intended to rival Bath. At Cheltenham, a pump house was constructed in 1738, but the spa really came to the fore in 1788 when it enjoyed the patronage of the visiting King George III, Queen Charlotte and a handful of royal princesses. And, of course, there was Bath itself, where the first pump room was opened in 1706, with a second one being constructed in 1795.

Spa towns prospered because of the perceived health-giving properties of the water. In particular, childless women were encouraged to 'take the waters' in order to settle their nerves and to prevent spasms of the womb. The craze started to diminish after 1800 when the apparent benefits of sea water came into vogue, and Bath and other spas were soon overtaken by the coastal resorts such as Brighton.

Finally, no investigation of libido-enhancers and conception-boosters would be complete without reference to Dr Graham's Temple of Hymen and Health. Sophie von la Roche remarks that she was surprised to see this noble emporium in such a neighbourhood (St James's) after waxing eloquently about the grazing cows and fallow deer cropping the grass in the meadows there. That was in 1775, and she noted that by 1781 it had moved to Pall Mall.

The ideas showcased in Dr Graham's Temple scream 'eighteenth century', whereas all the lotions, potions and procedures described above are merely variations on medieval folklore. The Temple reflected the new ideas about the therapeutic qualities of electricity, of the wonderful properties of magnetism, of the soothing properties of heavenly music, gentle lighting and sweet smells. But it was all a complete hoax, peddled by a quack called John Graham. He had been born in Edinburgh in 1745, dropped out of medical school without qualifying, and at some stage appears to have visited America where he met Benjamin Franklin and observed some of his experiments with electricity. When he came to Bath he joined the large number of men in that city selling miracle cures for the sickly rich; in his case, cures for lung disease and respiratory problems.

Graham could see the public obsession with sex and anything novel, and he moved to London in 1780 to open his Temple of Health and Hymen at the fashionable Adelphi. Before the whole idea is dismissed as quackery, Graham should at least get credit for recognising that sexual pleasure was not just about penetration, and not just about pleasing the man, but was just as enjoyable for the woman and that it was a sensual experience to be enjoyed even if procreation was not the ultimate aim. The public could come and listen to his lectures, drumming up business for the Temple, at which he extolled the virtues of electricity, propounded on women's rights, promoted vegetarianism, and drove home the qualities of exercise in the fresh air. Above all he promoted personal hygiene in an age when cleanliness was definitely not next to godliness. An example of his showman's style is shown in this flowery prose on the topic of genital washing: 'two eyes of a dead sheep dangling in a wet empty calf's bladder, by the frequent and judicious use of the icy cold water, would be like a couple of steel balls, of a pound a piece, inclosed in a firm purse of uncut Manchester velvet!'

At the end of these lectures he would startle his audience in the front row by passing an electric current through the seats, leading to much jumping around and startled exclamations. If electricity could do this, what could it do to enhance the pleasures of the matrimonial bed? And what a bed! This 'medico, magnetico, musico, electrical' marvel apparently measured 12ft by 9ft. Above it was a vast dome that supported musical automata, fresh flowers and live turtle doves. The whole edifice sparkled with electricity, no doubt produced by someone hand-cranking a generator while hidden off-stage. The edifice was supported on forty glass pillars, and the inner frame of the bed tilted so that the man could 'follow his lady down-hill' to aid conception. Above, mirrors reflected the scene below, while a control panel released 'aethereal airs', heavenly perfume to arouse the senses. Magnets provided a 'sweet undulating, titillating, vibratory, soul-dissolving, marrow-melting motion,' while the movements made by the lovers themselves triggered organ pipes to exhale 'celestial sounds' with increasing intensity. What was not to like. And all for £50!

The public came to gawp and stare and soon Dr Graham was able to open another Temple of Prolific Hymen in Pall Mall. A one-way system had to be introduced to cope with the crowds. For those unwilling to pay for a whole night of untrammelled bliss there was the opportunity to enter the room and see the mighty bed, and no doubt to ogle at the barely-clad, beautiful young ladies who enhanced the view. One of the girls was rumoured to be Emma Hamilton, later to become famous as the mistress of one Horatio Nelson.

One thing distinguished Graham from other mountebanks of the time: he genuinely worried about infertility and the effects of what he saw as a declining population. Based on the wholly inaccurate figures produced by the Welsh preacher-come-statistician Richard Price in the 1770s, Graham was worried that Britain would be unable to fight its corner in Europe, let alone across the Atlantic where the population of the American colonies was rumoured to be doubling in size every couple of decades. Britain was, he surmised, in decline numerically, and he was on a crusade to do something about it. Mind you, he must have been impressed by the efforts of King George III, who seemed to be tackling the problem in a single-handed way, fathering fifteen children by his wife, Charlotte, during a period of just twenty-three years. For Graham, increasing the population was a patriotic duty, and there is little doubt that he genuinely believed that his miraculous bed could help supply the national need. With the backing of the glitterati of the day, such as the Duchess of Devonshire, his venture may have attracted crowds of onlookers, but ultimately there were not enough customers willing – or able – to cough up £50 for a single night between the celestial sheets.

Poor Dr Graham: the cornucopia of delights proved to be a financial disaster. He returned to Edinburgh and took to delivering lectures while buried up to his neck in mud. For him, earth-bathing gave him all the nourishment the human body needed, leading him to advocate the benefits of abstaining from food: totally. Perhaps unsurprisingly, he was dead by the age of forty-nine, an emaciated mentally-ill shadow of the great showman who had brought a touch of pizazz to London's sex scene just a few years earlier. Before he died, he attributed his financial failure to 'a too eccentric and too expensive imagination,' but in truth, he was just a man ahead of his time. Nowadays, it is easy to imagine that he would be an absolute sensation, with a cult following of eager groupies based just outside Tinsel Town.

Of course, in a world before trade misdescription legislation, it was easy for quacks to thrive. The newspapers of the day carried more advertisements for medical cures than almost anything else, and the cures related equally to impotence and venereal disease. In many cases the prescription was the same, and often as not involved exotica such as viper drops. The public popped their pills and quaffed their tinctures and the quacks went happily on their way. And perhaps not all the treatments were in vain: many contained significant quantities of alcohol and opium, one an analgesic and the other a euphoriant. Even if they did not make you better, at least they might make you feel better.

Dr Graham, one of the world's first sex therapists, giving one of his one shilling lectures.

Chapter 7

Ways of Avoiding Pregnancy: Including Contraception and Abortion

A few relevant statistics: in the 1700s the average age of women when they married was twenty-two, and for the men, twenty-six. Probably twenty per cent of women never married. Perhaps half of all marriages were ultimately childless, either because of fertility problems or because of infant mortality. An adult had roughly a one-

Casanova blowing up condoms to amuse the ladies, from a Victorian print dating from 1872.

in-three chance of ever being a grandparent, because statistically his or her children were likely either to die young, or not marry, or not have issue who survived. With figures like that you can see why George III had fifteen children, yet at the date of the king's death in 1820 he had only one legitimate grandchild (Victoria). In fairness, much of that was down to the Royal Marriages Act, which invalidated a number of his offspring's marriages. In an age when legitimacy mattered enormously to the wealthy – i.e. land-owning – classes, and not at all to the poor and those in rented accommodation, these figures led to significant class differences.

It has been estimated that in 1650 perhaps just one per cent of brides were pregnant at the date of their marriage. A hundred and fifty years later the figure had exploded, perhaps twenty-fold. Indeed, nearly a quarter of all first-born children were born outside marriage. It can be argued that the higher incidence of pregnant brides shows that more people were having pre-marital sex – or were less worried about the consequences – or were less pressured into having an abortion. For those at opposite ends of the social spectrum marriage had totally different connotations. For the rich, and for the aristocracy, marriage was about providing a legitimate heir. The age of consent for marriage in 1700 was twelve – later (in 1763) raised to sixteen – and it was not uncommon for a member of the aristocracy to marry a girl in her late teens when perhaps he was twice that age, had already 'sown his wild oats', been on the Grand Tour and so on, and was ready to settle down and produce an heir.

Contrast that with the other end of the scale, where it made very little difference whether the union was blessed by the church or not. The poor often 'married' by exchanging vows at the church door rather than having a ceremony officiated by the vicar, especially after 1695 when the State introduced a form of poll tax which included a tax on marriage ceremonies. The Marriage Duty Assessment was levied between 1695 and 1706 and gave a huge impetus to the idea of a common-law union. Before marriages had to be registered, before proper census returns, and, in cases where inheritance or property concerns were absent, perhaps as many as a half of all unions were not legally valid. Although a common-law wife was not married in the eyes of the law, and could have no property rights or rights on the death of her partner, she was nevertheless 'married in the eyes of God'.

So the question arises: how did a woman stop being locked into a continual cycle of getting pregnant and giving birth? And in particular how did she avoid getting pregnant before she married? After all, if a girl was likely to wait for eight years between menarche – say at the age of fourteen – and marriage, at say twenty-two, it would be naïve to think that only the one per cent who walked down the aisle when pregnant were the ones who had engaged in sex.

There were a number of sexual activities which could not, by their very nature, result in pregnancy: frottage, anal sex and oral sex being examples. Frottage, or frotting, are words which have today tended to be hijacked by the gay community, but in the sense of meaning non-penetrative mutual masturbation it can be applied to many cases where a couple achieved orgasm without risk of pregnancy. To frot – from the French *froter*, meaning to rub or polish – is different from frotteurism, which involves non-consensual rubbing between strangers. Frottage would have been popular especially if a young woman was anxious not to lose her virginity, or because the total absence of any exchange of fluids meant that there was a zero chance of pregnancy resulting. A higher risk was *coitus interruptus*, where the male penetrates but then withdraws at the last moment and ejaculates externally. It may have been common among married couples, but obviously required a high degree of self-control (and trust) and, of course, was not risk-free because spermatozoa can be found in the pre-ejaculatory fluid. Nevertheless, it was probably one of the most widely-practised forms of birth control.

Oral sex, known as fellatio when the act is performed on a penis, and cunnilingus when performed on female genitalia, was another alternative. Oddly, because of the total failure to understand the reproductive process, many people (even experienced lovers such as Casanova) were unclear if pregnancy could result from fellatio. In his *Memoirs* Casanova describes love-making with his favourite nun, a woman identified as MM (she has been given the probable attribution of Marina Morosini). Casanova whisked her away from her convent to a nearby luxury apartment on board his gondola, where she was apparently 'astonished to find herself receptive to so much pleasure.' On one occasion she swallowed a small amount of semen. Casanova lamented: 'I should be in despair if I happened to place you in a position to become a mother.' The nun replies that she would know before long, and describes how she might be 'cured' by a physician if she did indeed become pregnant. No explanation is given as to the nature of the 'cure' but this clearly demonstrates that abortion services were readily available, even for nuns!

Oral sex is mentioned but rarely in literature of the time. That is not to say that it did not happen, but the lack of slang words to describe it suggests that it was relatively uncommon, and whereas Grose's *Dictionary of the Vulgar Tongue* contains a huge variety of words to describe most sexual activities, oral sex is not one of them. Phrases such as 'sixty-nine' first appeared in English in the 1880s, whereas '*soixante-neuf*' had been used in France to describe an oral sex position as far back as 1790. 'Blow job' is a twentieth century word, even if 'blow' was in use 300 years ago meaning 'to bring to orgasm'. Other descriptions, from 'muff diving' to 'giving head' and 'going down on', are all recent creations. Even 'fellatio' did not come into common use until 1894. Back in the nineteenth century there were references to 'prick eating', 'minetting', 'gamahuche' and 'eating seafood', but in previous centuries such words probably did not even exist.

There was something decidedly 'French' about oral sex, and perhaps this reflected disquiet about a practice which involved intimacy at a time when personal hygiene was often non-existent. *Harris's List* contains an occasional reference to licking, as in the 1788 edition which informed readers that Miss Noble at No. 10, Plow Court, Fetter Lane, 'has a most consummate skill in reviving the dead; for as she loves nothing but active life, she is happy when she can restore it: and her tongue has a double charm, both when speaking and when silent; for the tip of it, properly applied, can talk eloquently to the heart, whilst no sound pervades the ear and send such feelings to the central spot, that immediately demands the more noble weapon to close the melting scene.'

By the following year the List had included Miss H—lsb—ry, of No. 14, Goodge Street. She was apparently a finely made young lady, with a prepossessing countenance, and expressive dark eyes: 'She may, in more senses than one, be pronounced a great linguist. A velvet salute of this kind, had nearly disgusted Lord L—; but having got over the first impression, he found that her tongue was attuned to more airs than one;

but she never admits either of her mouths to be play'd with for less than two guineas.'

But if Harris was coyly using terms like: 'She is as talented silent as she is when she speaks,' French trade directories were far more open about fellatio. It rather looks as though in Britain the underlying religious teaching that 'sex was wrong unless it was to do with procreation', coupled with hygiene issues, turned people against oral sex. There are occasional references to men having oral sex with other men, such as a case brought before the courts in 1704 when John Norton was accused of taking hold of the privates of John Coyney and of 'putting them into his mouth and sucking them'. Also, many of the illustrations used in later editions of Cleland's *Memoirs of a Lady of Pleasure* feature oral sex, but by and large it was as rarely described as anal sex. Again, this would have fallen foul of puritanical objections to 'sex for sex's sake'. Fanny Hill makes a reference to anal sex when describing an encounter with an enthusiastic sailor, saying: 'he leads me to the table and with a master hand lays my head down on the edge of it, and, with the other canting up my petticoats and shift, bares my naked posteriors to his blind and furious guide; it forces its way between them, and I feeling pretty sensibly that it was not going by the right door, and knocking desperately at the wrong one, I told him of it:—'Pooh!' says he, 'my dear, any port in a storm.' Nevertheless, he immediately withdraws.

For aficionados of anal sex, *Harris's List* of 1773 recommended Betsy Miles, of Old Street, Clerkenwell. She was apparently known for: 'her immense sized breasts, which she alternately makes use of with the rest of her parts, to indulge those who are particularly fond of a certain amusement [...] backwards and forewards, are all equal to her, posteriors not excepted, nay indeed, by her own account she has most pleasure in the latter. Very fit for a foreign Macaroni — entrance at the front door tolerably reasonable, but nothing less than two pound for the back way. As her person has nothing remarkable one way or the other, we shall leave her for those of the Italian gusto'.

Short of 'alternative' sex, how else might a couple avoid pregnancy? Obviously, the rhythm method may have been used, i.e. a reliance on avoiding sexual intercourse on the days when the woman was ovulating. However, in an era of incredible ignorance about bodily functions it seems unlikely that many women would have felt happy relying on 'Vatican roulette'. Doctors simply did not understand the mechanics of ovulation, let alone the precise timetable involved. Far more common would have been a reliance on breastfeeding as contraception, especially among lower class families. Here, the woman was much more likely to offer her services as a wet nurse to infants born to wealthier families, and thereby prolong the period of time before she resumed menstruating.

Modern studies of what is called the lactational amenorrhea method (LAM), i.e. breastfeeding in order to avoid ovulation, show that the contraceptive effect of LAM is comparable to that of using a modern condom. During the first six months of a baby's life the constant sucking by the baby causes progesterone levels to remain suppressed. No progesterone, no ovulation; no ovulation, no period, and no pregnancy. It is only effective if breastfeeding takes place at least every four hours during the day, and every six hours at night, and whereas eighteenth-century women would not have any idea what LAM was, or how it worked, in an era before dried milk compounds and a modern move away from breastfeeding, women instinctively relied on a method which they could tell was remarkably effective.

It is also the case that malnutrition caused many women to be less fertile. Poor diet could lead to conditions such as pre-eclampsia, low birthweight, neonatal hypocalcemia, poor postnatal growth, bone fragility, and increased incidence of auto-immune diseases. All are linked to low vitamin D levels during pregnancy, reducing the chances of a woman having a successful pregnancy and giving birth to a healthy child.

What then of contraceptive methods, and abortifacients? The answer is complicated by the fact that whereas we see a distinction between contraception (avoiding pregnancy) and abortion (getting rid of the foetus) there was no such distinction either in law or in the minds of the general public in the eighteenth century. Terminating a pregnancy before 'quickening' occurred was not a criminal offence. The great legal commentator Sir William Blackstone declared that 'Life [...] begins in contemplation of law as soon as an infant is able to stir in the mother's womb'. A first-time mother might expect to feel the first signs of movement after around eighteen weeks; other mothers might feel movements two or three weeks earlier. It meant that in law a woman was not guilty of infanticide if she aborted the foetus during those first three months of pregnancy. The first time Parliament tried to legislate against abortion was in 1803 with the passing of the Malicious Shooting or Stabbing Act. This clarified the law relating to abortion and stated that it was an offence for any person to perform or cause an abortion. Under section 1, the punishment for performing or attempting to perform a post-quickening abortion was the death penalty, whereas Section 2 made it illegal, for the first time, to cause an abortion of a pre-quickening foetus. In the latter case the crime was a misdemeanour, punishable by a fine, imprisonment, the pillory or whipping – or a combination of such penalties – or up to fourteen years transportation.

Prior to this legislation there was no particular sanction against abortion and an unwanted pregnancy could be 'got rid of' either by using an instrument inserted into the uterus, or by administering drugs, most commonly in the form of herbal abortifacients. Women would know well that violent purgatives could lead to a forced miscarriage. The herb pennyroyal (*Mentha pulegium*) when ingested, was known to induce abortion. Modern science shows that chemicals in the pennyroyal plant cause the uterine lining to contract and shed itself. Mind you, it could also lead to the lungs and nervous system being poisoned, cause liver and kidney failure, inflame the stomach lining, and ultimately kill the patient.

Aloes and turpentine were commonly used, along with laurel, madder, pepper and sage. Savin (*Juniperus sabina*) was highly poisonous but was used because it was felt that anything which caused a woman to be violently sick was likely to cause an abortion. In fact, there were over a hundred plants believed to encourage miscarriages. Many of them were identified by Nicholas Culpeper in *The English Physician* (also known as *The Complete Herbal*). The warning against taking these in pregnancy was a clear but coded reference to the fact that the herb was an abortifacient. Taking seven bay leaves might be given to 'a woman in sore travel of childbirth' in order to cause a speedy delivery. Culpeper expressly warned that the remedy should not be taken earlier in the pregnancy, 'lest they procure Abortment, or cause Labour too soon.' Advertisements and claims by quack doctors made it plain that their products were intended to 'remove female obstructions' and that delays in menstruation could be avoided by taking 'medical waters', a coded reference to the fact that the product was in fact intended to cause an abortion (in complete contravention of the warning that it should never be used if pregnant).

It would perhaps be unwise to follow Casanova's advice regarding abortion. On hearing that his friend, Giustiniana Wynne, was pregnant – and with her wedding to Andrea Memmo looming – she turned to Casanova for guidance. His recommendation? Having sexual intercourse with Casanova after he had smeared the tip of his penis with saffron and honey. Of course, the remedy did not work, which probably disappointed Casanova rather less than it disappointed Giustiniana, who went on to give birth to a boy in a convent outside Paris. Nowadays, Casanova's behaviour would probably be seen as rape – tricking a woman into having sexual intercourse on the strength of a lie does not make it consensual – but in the eighteenth century there was no room for such legal niceties.

Casanova is also credited with recommending fashioning a cervical cap from half a pulped lemon and inserting it in the neck of the cervix prior to intercourse. This physical barrier, combined with the spermicidal qualities of the acidic lemon juice may well have had some effect. Sponges soaked in vinegar were also widely used. The sponge may well have absorbed some of the semen, but the vinegar must have caused considerable discomfort and internal irritation.

Another of Casanova's recommended contraceptives involved placing a single gold ball in the neck of the cervix. In 1760 he wrote in his *Memoirs* that he had arranged for a goldsmith to make three such balls, one for each of the current ladies enjoying his favours. At first sight this may seem to have been an early form of 'jiggle ball' as featured in *Fifty Shades of Grey*, but actually it was thought that the ball would act as a physical barrier and prevent sperm passing.

Reverting to the sponge, this was a device favoured by many and when Jeremy Bentham wrote about the problems of reducing the birth-rate among the urban poor in his 1797 book *Situation and Relief of the Poor*, his advice was to insert a sponge into the vagina before intercourse. The need for controlling population numbers (especially among the poor) was famously proposed by Robert Malthus in his *Essay on the Principle of Population*, which was published anonymously in 1798. The whole topic of birth control took off and within twenty years Francis Place emerged as the forerunner in advocating contraception in one form or another. In the 1820s, shortly before the end of the Georgian era, Francis Place suggested that the use of the sponge was widespread, writing:

> What is done by people is this. A piece of soft sponge is tied by a bobbin or penny ribbon and inserted just before intercourse is to take place, and is drawn as soon as it has taken place. Many tie a piece of sponge to each end of the ribbon and they take care not to use the ribbon until it has been washed. If the sponge be large enough, that is: as large as a walnut or a small apple, it will prevent conception, and thus, without diminishing the pleasures of married life, or doing the least injury to the health of the most delicate women, both the woman and her husband will be saved from all the miseries which too many children produces.

It is perhaps worth noting that while advocating birth control, Place nevertheless fathered fifteen children by his first wife, Elizabeth Chad.

Regarding physical contraceptives, the condom was probably the least used. Described in more detail on page 88, one of the first times that the word 'condom' appears in the English language was in 1708 when John Campbell unsuccessfully asked Parliament to make the devices illegal. The Scots in particular saw it as an English device, a trick to reduce their natural fecundity.

The condom was always known to have some value in preventing pregnancy, even if its main use was to prevent venereal disease. So, in a poem dedicated to the condom and purported to be 'by the Revd. Mr Kennet, son of the late Bishop of Peterborough', and contained in a book entitled *The potent ally; or, Succours from Merryland*, we see it introduced first as a form of contraceptive:

> Cundum, which to thy altar nightly brings
> Ten Thousand vigorous unpolluted things.
> By this machine secure, the Willing Maid
> Can taste love's joys, nor is she more afraid
> Her swelling belly should, or squalling brat,
> Betray the luscious pastime she's been at'

It continues with the more common explanation that the condom prevented sexually transmitted diseases: 'Happy the man who in his pocket keeps, whether with green or scarlet ribbon bound, a well-made condom. He dreads not the ills of shankers or cordee or buboes dire.'

The writer even recommended wearing two condoms at the same time:

> But lest by chance some direful flaw should Spring
> From hasty thrust and vigour of thy thing
> Do as sage Ch..s..l..n is wont to do
> For extra safety put on two.

The same poem in a slightly different form reappeared in *The Machine, Or Love's Preservative*, printed three years later.

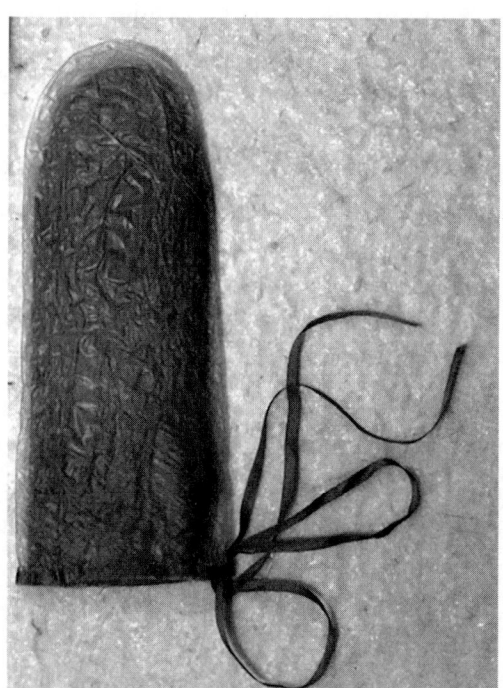

Condom made from animal gut, traditionally tied with a pink ribbon.

Chapter 8

Sexually Transmitted Diseases and their Treatment

If there was one corollary to the sexual openness of the eighteenth century that stands out, it is venereal disease. No matter that medical opinion of the time failed to distinguish between gonorrhoea and syphilis, or scurvy come to that; no matter that doctors thought that venereal disease resulted from men having sex with impure women (never the other way round); no matter that the usual prescription recommended for treating venereal disease was based upon mercury, a ghastly treatment that killed before it cured.

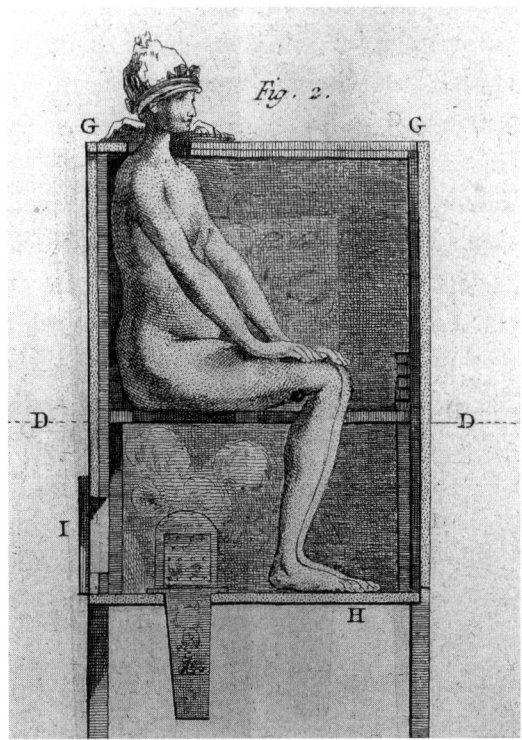

A sufferer from venereal disease experiencing the delights of being fumigated with mercury.

Venereal disease was rampaging out of control throughout the Georgian era. It shamed the innocent as well as the guilty: the 'pure' wives and girlfriends given the disease by partners who had slept with diseased whores; the whores themselves; the errant males who slept away from home; the innocent babies born with the disease. It was a disease associated with shame and secrecy, with humiliation and public condemnation. And yet, to read the literature of the time and to see the art and caricatures from the period, you would think that prostitution was a walk in the park, that roués and rakes could laugh off the sickness as a badge of honour; a sign of how many conquests they had enjoyed. Read John Cleland's *Memoirs of a Woman of Pleasure*, or Defoe's *Moll Flanders* and you could be mistaken for thinking that life was a bowl of cherries, and that harlotry was unmitigated fun. Read Henry Fielding's *Tom Jones* and you get a riotous romp, not a tale of disease and despondency.

Almost alone, William Hogarth pointed out the misery and suffering, affecting young and old, male and female, virtuous and amoral, which resulted from syphilitic infections. His series of paintings such as *Marriage a la Mode*, his *Rake's Progress* and his *Harlot's Progress* all demonstrate the inevitable downward spiral into disease and death for those who led a life of licentiousness. But Hogarth apart, you rarely see writers or artists portraying the true cost, paid particularly by Londoners, as they stumbled their way through the nightmare of venereal disease.

Research carried out by Simon Szreter, Professor of History and Public Policy at St John's College, Cambridge University, suggests that in the city of Chester in the 1770s a not insignificant eight per cent of the population aged under thirty-five were infected by syphilis, with numbers roughly equal between the sexes. Yet, beyond a radius of ten miles of Chester city centre, the incidence dropped to just one per cent.

It is, of course, unwise to read too much into the figures from just one area, but this suggests a far higher incidence of promiscuity – and hence infection – in urban areas. It is also safe to assume that London, with its vast number of brothels and bagnios, would have had an even higher percentage of infected adults. A look at admission records belonging to the city's main public hospitals, St Bartholomew's and St Thomas', suggests that in some years between twenty and twenty-five per cent of all admissions may have been linked to the treatment of venereal disease.

Syphilis as a cause of death is hard to calculate, because although there were Bills of Mortality published regularly for all persons dying within the city boundaries, the cause of death, ascertained by elderly 'searchers', was often unreliable. The wealthy would ensure that the shame of 'death by French Pox' would not appear alongside the name of their recently deceased. Probably only the parish paupers were recorded as having died from venereal disease; the rest were shown as having succumbed to some undefined 'ague or fever'.

The problem with syphilis is that it is a great imitator: it shows symptoms that are easily confused with other illnesses, making it easy for it to be confused, in its early stages, with ailments such as scurvy. Both syphilis and gonorrhoea were seen as distempers caused by too much heat in the blood. Gonorrhoea, otherwise the clap, was seen as a sort of junior version of syphilis (known as the pox), and something more minor. It was not until 1838 that Philippe Ricord, a physician and surgeon, firmly established that syphilis and gonorrhoea were separate diseases. Earlier confusion extended to muddling venereal disease with scurvy because scurvy, like gonorrhoea in its later stages, could exhibit rashes, pustules and chancres.

Syphilis and gonorrhoea were diseases regarded as having been spread by intercourse with infected women. The man was generally regarded as blameless in passing it on. Thus a man might wear a condom, but that was to stop him getting infected, not to stop him spreading the disease. For that reason, a husband was most unlikely to wear a sheath when making love to his wife; to do so would be to imply that she was the source of infection. In this way ignorance fashioned hypocrisy: that it was OK for men to sleep around, while the appetites of wanton whores should be kept in check lest they infect the good honest Englishman going about his business and having fun.

Syphilis knew many names: it was the French Pox, the Great Pox and the Neapolitan Disease (after the virulent outbreak of disease among French soldiers after they occupied Naples in 1495). The disease often led to a whitish discharge from the genitals, known as 'whites' in women, 'gleets' in men or 'running of the reins' in both sexes. Such discharges were regarded as being gonorrhoea and were believed to have been caused by masturbation and not just by sexual intercourse. Indeed, it was thought that problems with the lower back area – perhaps as a result of an accident or undisclosed illness – could also lead to gonorrhoea. We now know that gonorrhoea is caused by a bacteria called *Neisseria gonorrhoeae* or *gonococcus*, and in many cases it is passed on by someone who has no idea that they are infected. One in ten men, and perhaps half of all female 'sufferers', do not exhibit the usual symptoms (in particular, sores and genital discharges). By the time they are aware that they have the disease, it has already been 'passed on' down the chain of sexual partners.

Syphilis on the other hand is caused by a different bacteria (*Treponema pallidum*, if you really want to know) and victims go through four separate stages, from genital ulcers through to rashes and joint pains, and then to a latent stage where no new symptoms appear, sometimes for several years. This latter phase was particularly misleading because it made people feel that they had been 'cured' of the disease. Doctors and quacks alike could point to the suspension of symptoms as proof that their treatment had worked. However, in many cases the infection led eventually to foul-smelling abscesses and pocks all over the body. The sores would become ulcerated and in turn eat into bones and destroy the flesh around the nose, eyes and mouth. The combination of the smell and the unsightly ravaging of the face meant that it was a disease which could not simply be passed off as something minor. Sufferers were ostracised and often shut away in places such as the London Lock Hospital, which opened its doors to the public at the end of January 1747 at Grosvenor Place. The hospital had a strict rule than patients, once discharged, could never be readmitted. This was unhelpful, given that many of the female patients had no skills to fall back on to make a living, and therefore resorted to prostitution, leading to re-infection. To combat this, the Lock Asylum for the Reception of Penitent Female Patients opened at 5–6 Osnaburg Row in 1792 as a refuge for women who had been treated in the Lock Hospital. Here, they would have been given training in one of the needle trades, such as tailoring, embroidery and lace-making: enough for them to eke a living away from prostitution.

Prior to the 1700s there were a variety of ideas as to what caused syphilis and its rapid spread across society. David Turner, in his 1717 book entitled *Syphilis: a practical dissertation on the venereal disease* dismisses the old idea that it was a disease originally caused by 'the natural

Conjunction of a leprous Man with a menstruous Woman, or from the unnatural or sodomitical, of another with a diseased Beast, from Poison'd Wine; the influence of some malevolent star, or the venomous bite of a Serpent.' He also wrote that he was not convinced that it could be caught by 'common Conversation, drinking after one, sitting on the same Close-Stool, drawing on a Glove, or by wiping on the Napkin or Towel, after the infected person.' Opinion had moved on, and Turner thought that it might be caused by 'kissing, by the lips; suckling, by the nipple; Sweating in Bed with an infected Person; by the pores; but generally, in impure Embraces.'

For a young man looking for some action, how was he to guard against getting infected? Obviously choosing a virgin might be a good start, or he could follow the advice offered by John Browne in his 1703 book *The Surgeons Assistant* which lays the blame firmly at the feet of beautiful women. In his words: 'Those who do mostly exercise themselves [...] with impure Women, and do with most heat and lustful desire entertain them in their Embraces, they are seen sooner infected with this disease, than those that proceed with less vigour and heat.' In his view, this demonstrated the difference between 'those that are handsome and those that are ugly, where we may suppose, as the first by their charming Beauty may increase the flame, the other as ready is seen to extinguish it.' His logic runs something like this: the clap was caused by heat; passion causes heat; a man is likely to get more passionate making love to an attractive woman; therefore it is safest to choose an unattractive partner because she will not inflame you so much. Q.E.D.

Anyone wanting to take an attractive woman as a partner would be wise to make enquiries about her medical history, and in this context it is interesting to consult the diaries of James Boswell. Here was a man who meticulously chronicled his conquests especially when he was visiting London. Between the age of twenty and twenty-nine he had affairs with three married ladies, four actresses, kept three mistresses and cavorted with some sixty prostitutes encountered on the streets of the capital. In 1761 he described meeting a woman, to whom he gives the name Louisa (actually a Scottish actress called Anne Lewis). In due course they became lovers, but not before he had enquired about her health and medical history and was assured that she was free from disease. There is no mention of whether he disclosed to her that for his part he had already had several attacks of gonorrhoea. Since they were 'in the past' he did not see them as relevant. But after a while he writes: 'I this day began to feel an unaccountable alarm of unexpected evil: a little heat in the members of my body sacred to Cupid, very like a symptom of that distemper with which Venus, when cross, takes it into her head to plague her votaries.'

Outraged at what he saw as deliberate deception on the part of Louisa, he referred to her as a 'most consummate dissembling whore' and gave her the heave-ho, but not before he decided that she 'deserved to suffer for her depravity' and demands the return of two guineas he had lent her. He then writes: 'Thus ended my intrigue with the fair Louis, which I flattered myself so much with, and from which I expected at least a winter's safe copulation. It is indeed very hard. I cannot say, like young fellows who get themselves clapped in a bawdy house, that I will take better care again. For I really did take care. However, since I am fairly trapped, let me make the best of it. I have not got it from imprudence. It is merely the chance of war.'

It really is a wonderful insight into male attitudes towards sex: his own desires were perfectly normal, whereas for a woman they showed debauchery; his nasty little rash could only come from Louisa, and not reflect a re-occurrence of his earlier encounters with gonorrhoea; he felt cheated because he expected a whole season of love-making free from complications and she had denied him this. Presumably he felt 'conned' because if she had disclosed her earlier exposure to the disease he could have had the option of using a condom.

Condoms, originally made of linen but by the eighteenth century generally made from animal intestines, were often used as a method of avoiding sexually transmitted diseases. Condoms were sold by street walkers as well as in taverns, and were intended to be reusable. They had the disadvantage that they had to be soaked in water before use – to make them supple – and many users complained of the desensitising effect. As a barrier to the spread of disease they were not fully effective, not least because the animal gut was porous and bacteria could pass through. James Boswell describes a number of encounters with prostitutes; with some he wore what he described as 'armour' or 'his machine'. In particular on 31 March, he wrote: 'At night I strolled into the Park and took the

A gentleman, armed with a copy of Harris's List, calls at an address and now must make his selection. Harris's list; or, Cupid's London directory, 1794, by Richard Newton.

Whores dressing for a masquerade (see page 150). 'Dressing for a Masquerade' by Thomas Rowlandson.

The Chevalier D'Eon dressed as a woman and as a man. See page 151. 'Mademoiselle de Beaumont or, The Chevalier D'Eon'.

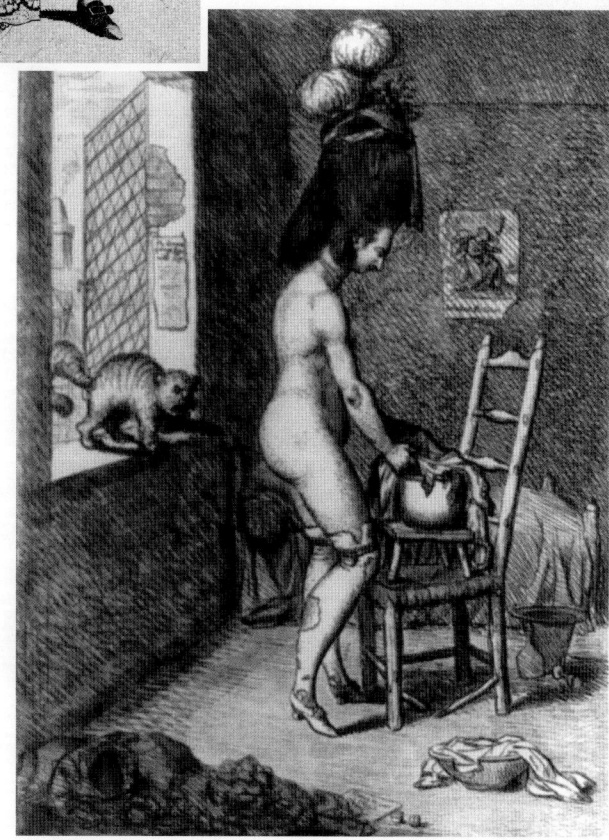

'The Whore's last shift' by James Gillray, 1779.

The Macaroni – a real character at the late masquerade. Mezzotint by Philip Dawe, 1773.

DILDO, an implement refembling the virile member, for which it is faid to be fubftituted, by nuns, boarding fchool miffes, and others obliged to celibacy, or fearful of pregnancy. Dildoes are made of wax, horn, leather, and diverfe other fubftances, and if fame does not lie more than ufually, are to be had at many of our great toy fhops and nick nackatories.

A dildo: dictionary definition. See page 52.

Cupid as a link boy by Reynolds. Link boys lit the way home, but also acted as rent boys. See Page 128.

Isaac Swainson promoting his 'Velno's Vegetable Syrup', facing an onslaught of rival practitioners advocating mercury. See page 93. *Mercury and his advocates defeated*, Thomas Rowlandson, 1789.

A Morning Frolic – or the Transmutation of the Sexes, by John Collet, 1782. See cross-dressing, page 146.

Plate V from Hogarth's *Marriage a la Mode*, by William Hogarth.

'The Cully Flaug'd' showing flagellation: 'an English vice'. See page 145.

'A fool and his money's soon parted'. Published by R Sayer, 1790.

From one end of the spectrum: 'A St Giles Beauty'. Printed by Carington Bowles, 1784.

From the opposite end of the spectrum: 'A St James Beauty'. Published by Carington Bowles, 1784.

Dr Rock selling his wares for treating venereal disease from a horse-drawn carriage at Kennington common, with John and Charles Wesley preaching in the background, 1743.

Dr Rock (seated) featured in the background of Plate 5 of William Hogarth's *A Harlot's Progress*. See page 92.

first Whore I met, whom I without many words copulated with free from danger, being safely sheeth'd. She was ugly and lean and her breath smelt of spirits. I never asked her name. When it was done she slunk off. I had a low opinion of this gross practice and resolved to do it no more.' Two weeks later he broke that resolve, recording on 9 April that he then: 'came to the Park and in armorial guise performed concubinage with a strong plump good-humoured girl, called Nanny Baker.'

What Boswell's diaries show is that he was a promiscuous young man of twenty-two who regarded it as perfectly acceptable to have paid sex with women who were often not particularly attractive, who he knew might well be infected, and who he felt safe with because he was wearing a condom. Afterwards, he occasionally felt shame at his behaviour and in one instance he writes: 'I determined to have nothing to do with Whores as my health was of great consequence to me.'

At times he had sufficient self-control to abstain from sex if no protection was available: 'I picked up a girl in the Strand and went into a court with intention to enjoy her in armour [i.e. wearing a condom]. But she had none. I toyed with her. She wondered at my size, and said "If I ever took a Girl's Maidenhead, I would make her squeak." I gave her a shilling; and had command enough of myself to go without touching her. I afterwards trembled at the danger I had escaped.'

He was not always so careful, writing: 'I sallied the Streets and just at the bottom of our own, I picked up a fresh agreeable young Girl called Alice Gibbs. We went down a lane to a snug place; and I took out my armour, but she begged that I might not put it on, as the sport was much pleasanter without it; and as she was quite safe. I was so rash as to trust her, and had a very agreeable congress.'

Boswell comes across in his diaries as being rather proud of his sexual prowess, and certainly shame never made him hold back from confiding about his sexual activities in his diaries. Catching venereal disease was a risk, but it was a risk worth taking as long as he had a condom.

When Casanova describes some of his many conquests he confirms his use of condoms, describing them by various names, from 'preservative sheaths' to 'assurance caps'. He describes one as an 'English riding coat [...] made of very fine and transparent skin, eight inches long and closed at one end, with a narrow pink ribbon through the open end.' He also describes a scene, in front of a group of ladies he was intending to seduce, in which they inflate the condoms to make sure that they were of good quality. By then condoms were being made out of a variety of materials, including oiled silk. By the 1780s advertisements referred to sheaths made from fish bladders; probably from the blow-fish.

But condoms were never universally popular, either with men or with women. A hundred years earlier Madame de Sevigny described the efficacy of condoms in a letter to her daughter, calling them 'an armour against enjoyment and a spider web against danger'. James Boswell also noted that they could be off-putting, with a diary entry in 1764 stating simply: 'Quite agitated. Put on condom; entered. Heart beat; fell. Quite sorry.' It is also worth remembering that Boswell describes catching a sexually transmitted disease, of one sort or another, on seventeen different occasions, suggesting that either he was not always careful, or that the condoms were pretty ineffective.

Doctors were well aware that promiscuity spread disease. Writing in his *Histoire de Ma Vie*, Casanova describes his return to the town of Orsera a year after his first visit. He is greeted enthusiastically by a local doctor, who credits Casanova with single-handedly developing his lucrative medical practice:

> It is to you, captain, to you (may God bless you!) that I am indebted for my present comforts ... You had a connection with Don Jerome's housekeeper, and you left her, when you went away, a certain souvenir which she communicated to a friend of hers, who, in perfect faith, made a present of it to his wife. This lady did not wish, I suppose, to be selfish, and she gave the souvenir to a libertine who, in his turn, was so generous with it that, in less than a month, I had about fifty clients.

One painting from 1779 by Johan Zoffany, entitled *Self Portrait with a Friar's Habit*, is unusual in that it shows a pair of air-drying condoms hanging on the wall. One suspects that it is not that the artist was hoping to get doubly lucky on a debauched night out, dressed in a masquerade outfit. The clue lies in the fact that the habit is one worn by Capuchin Franciscan monks, an order supported by Zoffany's one-time patron,

Ferdinand I, Duke of Parma. Ferdinand was equally famous for two things: his extreme religious devotion, and his equally extreme addiction to promiscuous sex. The two condoms mocked Ferdinand's sex life and were by no means a comment on his chosen method of family planning. They do, however, show the link between condoms and immoral behaviour.

And what of the young gallant who contracts a sexually transmitted disease, despite taking the precaution of wearing a condom, and even after getting his lover to answer a detailed questionnaire about her health, perhaps even carrying out a discreet examination to make sure that she is free from the trademarks of syphilis and gonorrhoea? What if he has chosen as his lover not the attractive object of his desire, fearful that she should overheat him, and instead chosen the ugly sister – not so attractive as to inflame his passions over-much – but still finds himself with a nasty dose of clap? Gonorrhoea or syphilis, the treatment was the same, and it usually involved mercury, hence the common saying: 'One night with Venus; a Lifetime with Mercury'.

By the 1700s it was already apparent to many that mercury was not only ineffective, but also caused terrible side-effects, including death. That did not stop its use, and Turner's *Practical Dissertation*, mentioned earlier, was reprinted in 1724, 1727, 1732 and 1737 and continued to extol the virtues of mercury. The patient had to allow for treatment lasting over one month, during which time he would be shut away in a hot, humid room or small, airless cupboard. This type of fumigation remained in use well into the nineteenth century. Mercury ointment would be rubbed into his skin several times a day and the patient would be made to lie next to a roaring fire in order to bring on profuse sweating. Some doctors added vitriol and arsenic to the mix. The side-effects included severe mouth ulcers, loss of teeth, nerve damage and kidney failure.

Some medical practitioners favoured injecting calomel, otherwise known as sweet mercury. It could also be taken orally. Others favoured mercuric chloride, despite its corrosive effect, and the patient would spend weeks stuck in his place of confinement while being forced to inhale vapours from the mercuric chloride, laced with heated cinnabar and metallic mercury. Cinnabar was a combination of mercury and sulphur; the patient would sit on a commode once the cinnabar had been placed underneath, on a hot iron.

Many doctors advised against using mercury in high doses. The Scottish physician Dr William Buchan had written his influential *Domestic Medicine* in 1769. It was a phenomenal success, selling over 80,000 copies, spread over nineteen editions, before he died in 1805. He recommended that treatment should start with astringent injections made from white vitriol, sometimes combined with cooling purges and enemas. For those patients who 'preferred an electuary' (in other words, a medicinal compound made more palatable by having been mixed with honey, or otherwise sweetened to taste) he recommended the following: 'Take of the lenitive electuary four ounces, cream of tartar two ounces, jalap in powder two drachms, rhubarb one drachm and as much syrup of pale roses as will serve to make up the whole into a soft electuary.'

Buchan also recommended that the patient should either have a poultice administered, or wear a truss: 'Few things tend more to keep off inflammation in the spermatic vessels, than a proper truss for the scrotum. It ought to be so contrived as to support the testicles, and should be worn from the first appearance of the disease till it has ceased some weeks.'

It would appear that Dr Johnson's friend, Hester Thrale, a prominent blue-stocking, followed Buchan's advice when her husband got the pox. As she put it: 'Mr Thrale told me that he had an ailment and he "revea'ld a Testicle swelled to an immense size."' She continued, in her diary: 'My poor father's prophecy was verified who said if you marry that scoundrel he will catch the pox and for your amusement set you to make his pultices. This is now literally made out and I am preparing pultices as he said, and formenting this elegant Ailment every night and morning for an hour together on my knees.'

Buchan had this to say about mercury: 'It must be acknowledged that mercury, taken inwardly for any length of time, greatly weakens and disorders the bowels for which reason, when a plentiful use of it becomes necessary, we would prefer rubbing to the mercurial pills.' The ointment was to be applied last thing at night, to the insides of the thighs. Having cold baths helped, as did drinking claret or other red wine adulterated with spa water.

It is clear that throughout the century different doctors came up with different plant extracts to be used alongside mercury. Buchan mentions china-root, the roots of soap-wort and burdock, and something called guaiacum (an ingredient still used in homeopathy). Doctors recommended sarsaparilla (still used as a diuretic and to treat skin ailments) along with the wood of sassafras (used nowadays, in conjunction with sarsaparilla as the main ingredient of root beer). Another plant, the mezereon root (the spurge laurel, or paradise plant) was often used. But above all, mercury was the basis of all treatments recommended by the good doctor, although he advised against its use by women who were menstruating, or by women in the final stages of pregnancy. Less happily, he felt that: 'if the woman be not near the time of her delivery, and circumstances render it necessary, mercury may be given but in smaller does and at greater intervals than usual – with these precautions both the mother and the child may be cured at the same time.'

Doctors became keenly aware that the 'cure' using mercury could be worse than the disease. By the early years of the eighteenth century experiments were made using other ingredients, with the English surgeon William Wallace introducing iodine therapy, using potassium iodide. Much later, gold, platinum and vanadium were tried, but without success.

William Wallace deserves a mention, although strictly speaking his experiments took place in the late Georgian period. He died in 1837, but not before he had demonstrated the infectious nature of syphilis by injecting 'secretions from the exanthematic sores' from a couple of secondary stage patients into three healthy recipients. They too caught syphilis, but were 'succesfully cured' of the disease, using mercury. Medical experiments of this nature were illegal even in those days, but the fact that Wallace was happy to publish his findings shows that ethics played hardly any part in medicine in the Georgian era.

It was small wonder that many sufferers felt unwilling to commit to a whole month of fumigation. (Can you imagine going to see the boss and explaining that you did not think that you would be coming into work for four or more weeks while you went to sit in a hot room working up a sweat?). Or even worse, for a woman infected by her errant husband, facing the shame and humiliation of being treated by a male physician, and having to submit to horrendous and intrusive treatments. No surprise that many sufferers would clutch at straws and try their hand at quack remedies, of which there was an inexhaustible supply.

To the eighteenth-century mountebank, the epidemic of venereal disease was manna from heaven, a chance to peddle all manner of wondrous treatments to a gullible public. There were few more famous than Dr Rock. A 1755 edition of the *London Gazette* commenced with the announcement that: 'By the Kings Patent: His Majesty having been graciously pleased to grant his Royal Letters Patent, bearing the date at Westminster 17 October 1751 in the 25 Year of the Reign, unto Richard Rock, of the Parish of St Bridget [...] licentiate in Medicine, for his new compound Medicine, or Anti Venereal Cathartick Electuary, for the true cure of fresh venereal injuries and all the lurking relicts or remains of old ones.'

The public could call on Dr Rock at the sign of the Golden Head and Key at Ludgate Hill in London and hand over their six shillings and receive a pot of the miraculous cure-all, together with a 'Book of Directions'. This was the same Richard Rock who features in two of William Hogarth's etchings: one called *Morning* – the first of his *The Four Times of the Day* – in which Rock is selling his anti-venereal pills in Covent Garden, and the other in the fifth scene in the *Harlot's Progress* where he is shown arguing with another well-known quack by the name of Dr John Misaubin while their patient lies dying from venereal disease. It is shown at Plate 8.

Newspapers of the day were full of medical advertisements, the majority of them for treating venereal disease. Leake's Pills were prepared and sold by Thomas Taylor, a member of the Corporation of Surgeons, at 9 New Bridge Street. At a cost of 2s. 9d. a box, these were promoted as being, 'justly famous for curing, in all its stages, the Venereal Disease. One small pill is a dose. One box in a recent case brings speedy recovery. It will effect a cure when salivation and other methods all avail nothing.' The claim was that 40,000 people of both sexes had been cured in the eight-year period up to 1791.

Or the public might invest its hopes in buying Dr Arnold's Pills, which were to be bought for one guinea a bottle at the doctor's house at Number 7 Gough Square, Fleet Street. The advertisement promised that 'though mild and innocent in their nature they [the pills] have been found by long experience to be an invaluable remedy for the venereal disease and have effected a cure where salivation would fail.' The pills were intended for use by 'those who have injured themselves by intemperance, and young people who feel in the prime of life the dreadful effects of a secret vice.'

Then there was everything from viper oil to Velno's Vegetable Syrup. The latter herbal remedy was promoted so successfully by the botanical gardener Isaac Swainson that he supposedly made £5,000 a year from its sales. Rather than limiting himself to claiming a cure for venereal disease he also maintained its efficacy in treating leprosy, gout, scrofula, dropsy, small pox, consumption, tape worms, cancer, scurvy, and diarrhoea. He is shown in image Plate 4 facing an onslaught from those physicians who still advocated mercury as a cure-all.

The Martyrdom of Mercury.

Chapter 9

Rape

In a century where crimes against property – such as stealing a pocket watch – were regarded as so heinous that they merited the death penalty, crimes against the person were frequently looked on as lesser offences. Nevertheless, until 1841 a conviction for rape carried the death penalty. The very severity of the punishment may often have made a conviction harder to achieve and often the lesser charge of an assault with intent to rape was preferred. In such cases witnesses were thought more likely to give evidence than on a capital charge. More to

Hogarth's 'The Harlot's Progress', showing, in the doorway, the loathsome image of the 'Rape Master General' Colonel Charteris.

the point, gaining a conviction for rape was extremely difficult. It was not just a case of 'her word against his'; that would have suggested a level playing field where the evidence of the woman was awarded equal weight with that of the man. Far from it, because in the eighteenth century the woman's testimony was tainted by the assumption that a woman had little or no control over her own carnal desires, that she could always have prevented rape if she had kept her legs crossed, and that women were congenital liars.

In an extraordinary book on jurisprudence, published in 1787 and entitled the *Elements of Medical Jurisprudence*, author Samuel Farr put forward the view that rape was an impossibility. No matter that the victim may have been terrified out of her wits, or have been held at knifepoint. He also suggested that women were incapable of telling the truth, adding that 'it may be necessary to enquire how far her lust was excited, or if she experienced any enjoyment.'

If so, it followed that she was only alleging rape after the event in order to try to conceal her shame and wickedness. Farr, a qualified physician, went further, stating that if pregnancy resulted from the alleged incident this was in itself proof that sex was consensual 'for without an excitation of lust, or the enjoyment of pleasure in the venereal act, no conception can probably take place.' Farr was merely stating a view which has echoed down the centuries: that women were 'asking for it' and that they were themselves to blame for the rape. He went on to propound the belief that rape was a physical impossibility, 'For a woman always possesses sufficient power, by the drawing back of her limbs, and the force of her hands, to prevent the insertion of the penis into her body.' This from a man who held himself out as being an expert witness in criminal trials, and who advised others on giving evidence in court.

Force was regarded as central to the allegation of rape and surgeons therefore set great store in finding evidence of bruising or abrasion around the genitalia, conveniently overlooking the fact that the man may have held a knife to the girl's throat at the time, or had threatened to strangle her.

Learned opinions about penetration were sought. In the case of the alleged rape of the seven-year-old Mary Tabor: 'John Brown deposed, that he viewed the Child with two other Surgeons, that there was not a Penetration large enough for a Man to make; that he try'd with a Probe, which would not go up; that she had a Running, and that he had known the like Hurt occasion'd by a Child's Riding on a Horse. Another Surgeon that was with the Child at the same time as the former, deposed that there was no Penetration large enough for a Man, that she was not lacerated, and that the Probe would not enter.' This, despite the fact that she had caught venereal disease as a result of her encounter with William Robbins, who was acquitted in 1721.

The same sessions of the Old Bailey noted that: 'Daniel Collins, of St. Paul at Shadwell , was indicted for committing a Rape on the Body of Mary the Wife of Henry Powell. But no Evidence coming against him, and it appearing to be a Contrivance to extort Money from him, the Jury Acquitted him.'

It was one of many cases where the defendant alleged that the accusation was made in order to extort money. In one particular case a man called George Carter was indicted for the rape of a servant maid at the Old Bailey in 1772. She was said to be 'a poor girl, without father, mother or friends, and that she came from Wiltshire, and that she had lived in different services in town till she went to take up employment in the prisoner's home'. He raped her, and afterwards paid her sixpence to keep quiet. She went to complain to the wife of the prisoner, who announced that 'he always served all his servants so, the first night they came into his house', and gave her another sixpence. Later she was prevailed upon to withdraw an allegation of rape – upon being paid a few shillings – before deciding to press ahead with the complaint. In court the girl was asked if she expected to be recompensed financially if the rape was proved, and on hearing that she hoped to make six or seven guineas out of the incident, the defendant was acquitted despite all the evidence against him.

Rape technically involved penetration without consent, but in many cases the courts looked for a second piece of evidence: ejaculation. In after-the-event examinations, learned doctors would solemnly announce that there was no trace of semen; therefore there had been no intercourse, and the woman was not telling the truth. Conversely, soiled sheets might aid a conviction, as would the evidence of any third-party rushing in unexpectedly and viewing the incident.

Add to this the fact that the poor woman was often humiliated and embarrassed at having to give evidence, and may well not have been familiar with using the language needed to describe the events which took place, and it is hardly surprising that eighty per cent of all rape trials at the Old Bailey failed to result in a conviction: the lowest conviction rate for all serious crimes. The complainant was often reduced to referring to what happened 'down there' or even 'the place where she made water'. And a young girl was hardly likely to be keen to discuss the loss of her virginity when to do so would seriously affect her chances in life, especially when it came to finding a suitable husband in the marriage market.

Reading the *Proceedings of the Old Bailey* for any given week in the eighteenth century reveals a whole litany of cases where, in a matter of minutes, prisoners were sentenced to death or transportation for offences which we would nowadays treat as misdemeanours. Next to those cases are reports where alleged rapists were acquitted because the evidence against the accused was uncorroborated, even in cases where the poor woman caught gonorrhoea as a result of the incident.

Take the case of Mary Marsh in July 1715. The trial proceedings state:

> William Cash, of the Parish of St. Martin in the Fields, was indicted for a rape committed upon the Body of Mary Marsh (a Girl of about 12 Years old) on the 17th of June last. It appear'd by the Evidence, That the Girl is Apprentice to the Prisoner's Wife ; That upon her complaining she was not well, she was search'd, and found to have a Gleet [in other words, a discharge caused by gonorrhoea] [...] The Girl swore, that about 7 o'Clock in the Morning of the same Day, she being starching, and her Mistress abroad, the Prisoner threw her upon the Bed, press'd her very hard, and put something into her, but was so modest she would not declare what. The Prisoner in his Defence had a Witness who swore, the Girl said he try'd, but could not enter her; and two Surgeons , who depos'd there had been no Penetration; and that the Gleet might proceed from a Strain, or Weakness, or ill Habit of Body. The Jury considering the Evidence on both sides, acquitted the Prisoner.

Medical examination of a woman's sexual organs was apparently relevant, with the *Elements of Medical Jurisprudence* listing instances where physical appearances were in themselves evidence of licentious behaviour. If a woman was of bad character, i.e. had previously had sexual intercourse out of wedlock, then her evidence could be disregarded. It was tainted, as was the case if she had any of the following physical attributes:

> The lips of the pudendum are flaccid and distended more than that of a maiden.
> The clitoris is enlarged, and hath a prepuce which covers the glans arising from constant friction.
> The nymphaea (labia minora) are also enlarged, and are of a lighter and more obscure colour.
> The orifice into the urinary passage is more open and exposed. This is owing to the flaccidity of the labia.
> The vagina is large and spacious.
> The wrinkles [of the vagina] are less prominent

So, if you had no wrinkles on your vagina, or an enlarged clitoris, you could not be a victim of rape. In the eyes of the law, prior sexual experience, as evidenced by such physical characteristics, counted against a woman. Her testimony could be dismissed and her character ruined. Small wonder that many rapes went unreported.

In a case against John Ellis brought before the Old Bailey in 1731, a witness was called to give evidence that the victim Sarah Matts was: 'a common vile Woman. The greatest Black-guard may lie with her for sixpence. I have seen her in Bed with a Man, in the Guard-Room, at St. James's. She always had the Character of a Whore and a Thief.' Another witness said that he had slept with the victim on a number of occasions, saying: 'I wanted a Bit of that same – as any other Man may – and so I invited her to the Sport, and lay with her in March and April too. I'll assure you I did not ravish her, otherwise than by talking her over, and making her drink, as a Man must always do in such Cases; for you know a Woman must be coax'd a little, though she's never so willing.'

The defendant was acquitted, despite evidence corroborating the victim's story: the men involved in the case clearly viewed all women as game, considered getting their victim drunk as part of the seduction process, and were determined to blacken her character afterwards in order to discredit her evidence. They were Jack-the-lads, she was a whore, and the court apparently accepted this.

It is hard to imagine the horror of having to give evidence before an all-male court. After all, the judges, the barristers, the court officials, the jury – everyone who the victim was likely to encounter – was going to be male. If she was sexually inexperienced, finding the right words to describe 'the thing' was going to be difficult if not impossible. Not for her the eloquence of John Cleland's Fanny Hill, describing testicles as 'globular fleshy eminences that compose the Mount Pleasants of Rome'. Fanny never used the word 'penis' – to her it was a 'mighty machine' – but to a shy, ill-educated and inexperienced rape victim appearing in front of a room of unsympathetic men it must have been almost impossible to articulate a convincing description of what happened.

You might think that cases involving paedophilia would be more straightforward, but unfortunately this was not the case because of the problems of a child giving evidence. Appalling cases, some involving children as young as five, were dropped because the child was too young to understand the nature of giving evidence under oath. In the trial of Regale Stewart he was charged with: 'ravishing and carnally knowing one Ann Merrick, a virgin, of the age of ten years ten months, against her will and consent, as well as ravishing one Ellinor Merrick, an infant of the age of four years and two months.' But evidence of actual penetration was not available, and the court refused to believe that the accused could have committed the offence, because he had fathered twenty-two children by his wife.

In another case, dating from September 1716, Mary Pewterer was charged with aiding and abetting the rape of a nine-year-old child. The case report stated: 'The Child, who was very little, depos'd that the Prisoner [...] took her out one Night to an Alehouse, and held her in her Lap, whilst a Man not yet known; abus'd her Person and gave her the Pox; and two Nurses of St. Thomas's Hospital swore, they never saw a Person more afflicted with that Disease that she had been. But the Jury not thinking the Evidence of so young a Child sufficient to convict the Prisoner, they Acquitted her.'

In another case it was held that a child under the age of ten could not take the oath: 'The Child being young the Court would not give her the Oath; and she being under the Age of Ten Years, had the Fact been Proved, it was not a Rape in the Eye of the Law, but an Assault, whereupon the Prisoner was acquitted.'

There were, of course, sometimes convictions of sex with young children. Take the case of William Kite in 1707. The trial report stated that Kite was indicted:

> for committing a Rape on the Body of Elizabeth Berry, a Virgin of 7 Years of Age, on the 21st of December last. The first Evidence was a Surgeon, who depos'd that he was sent for to inspect the Child's Body; That he found that a Male had been with her; That a large penetration was made, and the Foul Disease given her. The Child depos'd, that she being sent to the Prisoner's House for a pint Pot, the Prisoner took her and laid her cross a table, and gain'd the knowledge of her Body [...] The Evidence being positive, and the Prisoner saying little for himself, nor calling any to his Reputation, the Jury found him Guilty of the Indictment.

He was sentenced to death.

In a similar case involving a fifteen-year-old boy accused of raping a five-year-old girl called Ann Milton, James Peters gave evidence that:

> he liv'd in New Street, Shoe lane, and the prisoner came to live with him, in order to be bound Apprentice; and Ann Milton, a Neighbour's Child, coming to play with his Child, the prisoner took 'em up upon the Leads [i.e. onto the roof] where he lay with Ann Milton, and gave her the foul Disease. The Child complaining of her illness, occasioned the Fact to be discovered; upon which the prisoner ran away, and was not heard of till about a fortnight ago; when he was taken by John Milton , the Child's Father, at a Tobacconist's Shop in Shoe lane, near St. Andrew's Church, and being charg'd with the

Fact confest it. But when he came upon his Defence, at the Bar, said he knew nothing of the matter; and if ever he confest any such Thing, it was only in a fright. The Evidence being plain and positive against him, the Jury found him guilty of the Indictment.

What may also seem curious to modern eyes is that incest was not made a statutory offence until 1908. No matter that the Church laid down 'degrees of consanguinity' for marriage or that the general public treated incest with considerable distaste, it was not a criminal offence *per se*.

Cases involving incest in the eighteenth century were therefore dealt with as rape. Take the sad case of Mary Masland, thirteen years old, whose mother had caught venereal disease from her father and had had to be admitted to the Bedlam asylum. The girl had been sent into service, but when she lost her job she returned to the house of her father. According to the trial transcript the girl was then attacked by her father as she lay in bed: 'I cry'd out, and tho' he put a Handkerchief to my Mouth, yet a Boy that lay in the next Room heard me; and he gave me the foul Disease. I got up about Seven o'Clock in the Morning, and did not tell what had happen'd to any one, till about three Weeks afterwards; I was taken sick about that Time, and could neither walk nor stand; my Uncle carry'd me to a Surgeon.' Her story was corroborated by the servant boy in the next room, who heard the screams, and the medical evidence supported the girl's story. The trial reporter obviously felt that the medical evidence of incestuous rape was too disturbing to report fully, saying: 'The particular Circumstances were too shocking to be exposed; though unhappy Necessity call'd for a Declaration of Truth in the solemn Proceedings of Justice.' The prisoner's case was not helped by the fact that he went on the run and his defence seemed to consist of trying to persuade the court that he was positively angelic, 'If she has got the Foul Disease, I am innocent; for I am a clean Man; and if she is rotten with it, I am innocent as an Angel.' In the event, John Masland was found guilty and sentenced to death. History does not record what happened to his unfortunate daughter.

It has to be said: there was one law for the rich and one for the poor, as evidenced by rape allegations made against two particular members of the aristocracy. One involved the loathsome Colonel Charteris, who swaggered around proudly using the title of Rape Master General, and the other Lord Baltimore.

Francis Charteris was not just a rake, he was a rapist with a penchant for young servant girls. Jonathan Swift called him 'a most infamous, vile scoundrel'. He was a Scottish-born bully, a cheat and a confidence-trickster. He amassed a fortune through bribery, fraud and blackmail, and reputedly had an income of £7,000 a year, as well as £100,000 pounds invested in stocks and shares. Here was a man who apparently thought he could have any woman he wanted, under some twisted idea of '*droit de seigneur*'. On one occasion in Scotland he raped a married woman at gunpoint, before running away to England to avoid capture. In 1721 he petitioned the King (George I) for a pardon, and having obtained this he then felt safe to rape whoever and whenever he wanted. By his own claim, he had his wicked way with over 300 women. This thoroughly unpleasant man had no sense of honour and clearly regarded himself as being above the law. On one occasion, when staying at an inn in Lancaster, he reportedly persuaded a young servant girl to have sex with him on payment of a gold guinea. The next day, before departing, he told the inn-keeper that he had given the girl a gold coin and had asked her to have it changed into silver, and that she had failed to deliver his change. The girl was searched, the gold coin discovered, and of course the word of Colonel Charteris was accepted, and the girl's protestations were in vain: he got his guinea back, and she got the sack.

One of the drawbacks of his notoriety was that it was almost impossible to find female servants to work in his household, so when he needed a new servant-girl for his home at Hanover Square in London, he gave his name as Colonel Harvey. It was apparently part of a ritual, played out for the amusement of the somewhat fat fifty-four-year old colonel and his friends. Girls would be hired, raped, and then pushed out onto the streets. As the Newgate Calendar put it: 'His house was no better than a brothel, and no woman of modesty would live within his walls. He kept in pay some women of abandoned character, who, going to inns where the country waggons put up, used to prevail on harmless young girls to go to the colonel's house as servants; the consequence of which was, that their ruin soon followed, and they were turned out of doors, exposed to all the miseries consequent on poverty and a loss of reputation.'

William Hogarth had shown Charteris gleefully fondling himself while watching the arrival of the fresh-faced Moll Huckabout in the first plate of his series *A Harlot's Progress*. In October 1729 a young woman called Anne Bond was taken on as a maid-servant and was immediately besieged by the loathsome lothario. She resolutely declined the colonel's demands for sexual favours. On the third day she overheard someone refer to her master as Colonel Charteris. Realizing who 'Colonel Harvey' was, she sought to leave his employment immediately. He responded by having her locked in her room. The next day, 10 November 1729, he sent for her demanding that she make up the fire. He then brutally raped her, after gagging her screams with his night cap. When she stated her intention to report the crime, he had her stripped and horse-whipped, alleging that she was a thief. She was thrown out with no possessions.

Brave girl: she made a complaint against Charteris and initially he was charged with the misdemeanour of assault with intent to rape. The Middlesex Jury upgraded the charge to rape, a crime which carried the death penalty. The case was referred to the Old Bailey and the trial started on 27 February 1730. By then the trial was the subject of huge press attention. His defence team tried to besmirch Anne Bond's character, claiming that she was a prostitute and a thief. He claimed that the act was consensual, producing his household servants to give evidence that the girl was lying, and that they had heard no noises or screams at the time of the alleged offence. Charteris even produced a letter which his footman swore on oath came from the girl, but it was clearly a forgery. Three witnesses were produced to give evidence that Anne was a virtuous and religious young woman. The jury retired for just forty-five minutes to consider its verdict and on 2 March Charteris was found guilty and sentenced to death.

That should have been the end of the matter. He was carted off to Newgate prison and his goods were seized as being forfeit to the Crown. However, a campaign to pardon the appalling colonel soon got under way. It appears that he had 'friends in high places', including Robert Walpole, First Lord of the Treasury. He seems to have been able to buy off Anne Bond with the promise of an annuity of £800, enough for her to get married and open a public house: £15,000 was alleged to have been spent on 'oiling the wheels of justice' (in other words, laid out in bribes). It worked. Six weeks after sentence was handed down, George II granted a Royal Pardon, and the man was set free. He then had the nerve to sue for the return of his goods, even though his conviction as a felon meant that the seizure was entirely lawful. He ended up having to sell shares to obtain the return of his chattels. Meanwhile the press suspected that some of the £15,000 had been paid to Sir Robert Walpole as a bribe.

The public were outraged: the poor because it was a clear example that the rich could get away with anything, and the rich because he was a disgrace and a dishonest cheat. He was pilloried in the press with books such as *Some authentick memoirs relating to the life, amours ... of Colonel Ch----s. Rape-Master General of Great Britain*. A ballad entitled *On General Francesco, Rape-Master General of Great Britain* was published and he was attacked in print by popular writers such as Alexander Pope, John Arbuthnot and Jonathan Swift.

Charteris returned to Edinburgh in ill-health, possibly as a result of illness contracted in prison. He died on 24 February 1732. The outraged citizens of Edinburgh saw no reason why he should receive the full sacrament. They chased away the clergyman conducting the funeral, and pelted the grave at Greyfriars with manure, offal and dead cats. The despicable man never got the justice he deserved, and, assuming his boasts were correct, there were 300 young girls who were debauched and abandoned to a life of shame, poverty and, no doubt, early death. They are anonymous – apart from Anne Bond – but they are the true victims of justice in the eighteenth century.

Justice never featured too strongly in the life of Frederick Calvert, Sixth Baron Baltimore: a kidnapper, a rapist, a liar, but a free man. He had inherited his title, and vast swathes of Maryland, when he was twenty years old. Taking no interest whatsoever in his colonial heritage, he instead preferred to swan around Europe visiting Turkish brothels. He then decided to convert his stately pile into a Turkish-style seraglio, where he could keep his harem of mistresses. In 1753, when he was twenty-two, he married Lady Diana Egerton, daughter of the Duke of Bridgewater, but the marriage was a disaster and the couple separated in 1756. He was described at the time as 'a disreputable and dissolute degenerate' and also as being 'feeble in body, conceited, frivolous, and dissipated.'

He lived openly with a number of mistresses and became father to a small tribe of offspring, but even with his harem of willing concubines under his roof, he yearned for new conquests. He took a fancy to a young God-fearing Quaker girl called Sarah Woodcock, who was a virtuous young innocent living in London with her father. Lord Baltimore saw her while she was working in a millinery shop and took a fancy to her. She was lured to his home under false pretences, and once there, was imprisoned and threatened with violence unless she gave in to his Lordship's advances. Too scared to eat or drink in case she was being poisoned, she was kept a prisoner for four days until, weak and broken in spirit, she was raped by Lord Baltimore. He kept her in his house for a whole fortnight, raping her constantly, before her desperate father heard of her plight, found out where she was being kept, and secured a writ of *habeas corpus*.

Lord Baltimore's trial at Kingston Assizes was a sensation. He denied that Sarah was held under false imprisonment and claimed that sex was consensual. In essence his defence was no more than: 'It is her word against mine, and I am Lord Baltimore, son of a very distinguished father, and that should be good enough for the jury'. Amazingly, it was sufficient, and after eighty minutes of deliberation the jury acquitted him of all charges, as well as dismissing the cases brought against two of his employees who had been accessories.

Innocent in the eyes of the law maybe, but the newspapers generally sided with the humble milliner and savaged Baltimore for being an aristocratic debaucher who had behaved abominably and then tried to hide behind his rank and privilege. He suffered further embarrassment when Sarah Watson, one of the former members of his harem, published her memoirs under the title of *Memoirs of the Seraglio ... by a Discarded Sultana* (London, 1768). It contained many salacious details, eagerly lapped up by the public, including the suggestion that although he kept eight mistresses Lord Baltimore was not actually able to satisfy even one of them.

Lord Baltimore was driven into exile by all the adverse publicity. He caught a fever in Naples, and died on 4 September 1771, at the age of forty. Reflecting on the case, the Newgate Calendar commented, 'What shall we think of a man, of Lord Baltimore's rank and fortune, who could debase himself beneath all rank and distinction, and, by the wish to gratify his irregular passions, submit to degrade himself in the opinion of his own servants and other domestics?'

Others might think that degrading himself in the eyes of his servants was nothing compared to the wrong he did to a terrified Sarah Woodcock. Her reputation and her life were ruined and her story really does show that it was often the poor who paid the price for the rich man's fun.

The Bum Bailiff outwitted.

Chapter 10

Bigamy, Bestiality and Brothel-keeping

Bigamy

Marrying a second spouse while the first spouse was still living was a crime, but one that was not always clear-cut. Prior to 1753 marriages were not required to be registered, and because divorce was only for the wealthy, couples frequently split up and went their separate ways, later entering a second marriage in blissful ignorance as to whether the original spouse was still alive. In addition, there was much confusion as to the validity of some earlier marriages,

Elizabeth Chudleigh, Duchess of Kingston, brought into court on her trial for bigamy, accompanied by her chaplain, physician, apothecary and three maids of honour.

especially those entered into prior to Hardwicke's Marriage Act of 1753. A case in point was the courtesan Theresia 'Con' Phillips who married perhaps five or maybe seven times, but trying to work out which marriage was valid involved nearly twenty-four years of litigation. She had been raped at the age of twelve, married a man (who was probably already married) in order to escape from her creditors, married a second time, in the same church, two years later, had countless affairs, wrote her memoirs and, after spending time in various debtor's prisons, made her way to Jamaica where she died in February 1765.

In the absence of an official marriage certificate the court would look for evidence from neighbours as to whether a couple held themselves out as man and wife. The evidence was often trivial and circumstantial, but if proved, a common punishment was branding on the thumb. This punishment was administered in the courtroom at the end of the sessions in front of spectators. Bigamy could also lead to a custodial sentence, such as the six-month sentence in Newgate handed out by the Old Bailey in 1794 to bigamist Maria Edkins.

The majority of bigamy cases were brought against men and in the second half of the century there were over one hundred bigamy trials at the Old Bailey, of which eighty-six cases were against males. Fifty-five of the men were found guilty, and fifteen of them were branded. Thirty were sent to prison, seven were transported and in two cases the man got away with a fine.

Perhaps the most sensational bigamy trial of all time took place in 1776 and involved Elizabeth Chudleigh, who was either the Duchess of Kingston or the Countess of Bristol, depending upon which of her two marriages was valid. The press devoted endless column inches to the trial and its aftermath. To the lower orders it confirmed what they had always known: that their supposed social superiors were a load of lying degenerates. Many years later even *The Times* was moved to comment in June 1788 that, 'Bigamy, it seems, is a greater crime than simple fornication or fashionable adultery.'

Elizabeth had risen from fairly humble origins. The family owned a small estate in Devon, but they were not wealthy. Her father died when she was five, leaving her to be brought up in genteel poverty. Mother was forced to take in lodgers at her home in the newly developed, but not yet fashionable, area of Mayfair in London. Elizabeth had little formal education and was passed from pillar to post among distant relatives, until 1743 when her mother managed to get her a position at Court as Maid of Honour to Augusta, Princess of Wales. Elizabeth was twenty-two and desperately needed the £200 a year that went with the post. One day at Winchester Races she met and fell head-over-heels in love with a young naval officer called Augustus John Hervey. He proposed marriage almost immediately, but any marriage would automatically mean that Elizabeth would have to abandon her position as Maid of Honour (since married ladies were no longer considered to be maids). Hervey had little or no money of his own, and more to the point was about to leave on a two-year tour of duty.

Hervey was the second son of the Earl of Bristol, and his elder brother was alive, albeit in bad health. It was by no means certain that Augustus John would ever inherit either the title or the money that would go with it. However, the headstrong couple rushed into marriage, deciding to keep it a secret from the outside world. That way, she kept her position at Court, and he was able to avoid the risk of alienating his family. The wedding took place at Lainston in Wiltshire, on 4 August 1744, and he left to join his squadron, *en route* to the West Indies, two days later.

When the time came for Hervey to return to England, he found that his bride had not exactly been pining away during his absence. She had developed a close friendship with James, 6th Duke of Hamilton, and her flirtatious behaviour had attracted a host of other admirers, none of whom were aware of her marriage (marriage proposals from both the Duke of Hamilton and the Duke of Ancaster had been turned down).

Hervey was shocked and appalled at her reputation, and the couple did not even meet up for three months. It appears that Elizabeth was keen to see that her debts were paid by Hervey, but not so keen to have anything else to do with him. According to later reports, Hervey engineered a private meeting at his apartments by threatening to go public about the marriage if Elizabeth refused to see him. She turned up, was locked inside, and in the words of the time, 'he would not permit her to retire without consenting to that commerce, delectable only when kindred souls melt into each other with the soft embrace.' In other words, he forced himself upon her. The report continued, 'The fruit of this meeting was the addition of a boy to the human race.'

This was in 1747. In order to conceal the pregnancy Elizabeth discreetly moved to Chelsea where she could have the child, away from the prying eyes and ears of the Court. But the child, a boy, only lived a few months. The couple decided to separate a year after the birth, but, since the marriage was a secret, so was the news of the separation.

From that point in time, Elizabeth could no longer look to Hervey for financial support and protection, leaving her in a most vulnerable position. Her impetuous behaviour and lack of decorum caused difficulties at Court, but in time she befriended the shy but rather well-connected Evelyn Pierrepont, 2nd Duke of Kingston-upon-Hull. He was considered one of the most handsome men in England and by 1752 it was noted that the pair were an item. Their union meant that Elizabeth was able to spend money like water. A fine new house was built in London, called initially Chudleigh House, but later renamed Kingston House.

The question of her marital status became an issue. Hervey had settled in England and wanted a divorce, which could only be obtained by a private Act of Parliament. Such a step would inevitably mean public gossip and adverse comments in Parliament. If granted, the divorce would have meant that on any remarriage she would be seen to be 'second-hand goods'.

Elizabeth therefore objected to the whole idea of a divorce and instead petitioned the Ecclesiastical Court for a declaration that she had never been married. The onus was on Hervey to prove that the marriage had taken place, but whereas servants were produced to say that they had heard of the wedding, no one would testify that they had been present at the ceremony. Elizabeth swore blind that there was no such wedding. On 10 February 1769 sentence was pronounced, 'that the said Elizabeth Chudleigh was and now is a Spinster, and free from all matrimonial contracts and espousals with the said Augustus John Hervey.' A month later, on her forty-eighth birthday, Elizabeth married her duke.

Oddly, polite society turned against the couple. Everyone *knew* that she had been married, and whereas it was one thing to be the duke's mistress and be received at Court it was another to be seen as a flagrant bigamist. Elizabeth found herself shunned, and she and her husband retreated to his country estate. All was well for a few years, but the duke suffered a series of strokes and died in 1763. Under his will, everything passed to his widow, on condition that she did not remarry. Enter the jealous relations, outraged at either having to wait, or worse still, having been cut out of their inheritances altogether.

Meanwhile, March 1775 saw her first, and therefore legal, husband succeed to the Earldom of Bristol, making her the Countess of Bristol. It was not a title she wished to be known by, and in 1775 the Duke of Kingston's nephew, Evelyn Meadows, brought proceedings against her based on the fact that she had married bigamously. He wanted to set aside the will, either on the basis that there was no marriage, or that Elizabeth had used undue influence. In vain, Elizabeth sought to rely on the earlier decision of the Ecclesiastical Court. She also tried without success to get George III to intervene, or to help her get the case transferred to the House of Lords.

The bigamy trial in April 1776 was a sensation: Elizabeth was unwell and therefore escaped being locked up in the Tower prior to the trial. Instead, she was in effect put under house arrest. Some 350 tickets were printed granting entrance to the court. Even Queen Charlotte turned up one day. The general consensus was that Elizabeth would be found guilty, and there was much conjecture as to whether she could be sent to a penal colony, given that Britain was by then at war with her American colonies.

Witnesses who had previously denied the wedding suddenly appeared out of the woodwork and agreed that they had been present at the ceremony. Others, who might have helped Elizabeth, simply declined to give evidence or went on long holidays abroad. The result was inevitable. She was found guilty. The decision of the Lords was unanimous: 119 peers took it in turns to give a verdict of guilty. Only her rank (i.e. as Countess of Bristol) spared her from imprisonment. Instead she fled to the continent, her fortune intact but her reputation in tatters.

The question arises: was she a gold digger, a callous woman who lied through her teeth and enjoyed a status to which she had no entitlement? Or was she simply a woman who genuinely did not regard herself as being married (whatever the letter of the law) when she had spent so little time with Hervey as man and wife? Perhaps she had simply convinced herself that she was entitled to regard the order from the Ecclesiastical

Court as binding. Having been raped by Hervey, who can blame her? Certainly, she appears to have been a loving and devoted partner to the Duke of Kingston. He was clearly the love of her life, and vice versa. In the event it did not really matter. The public were able to indulge their appetite for scandal, gossip and intrigue, and the case sums up much about Georgian attitudes and hypocrisy towards marriage, infidelity, the courts and money.

Bestiality

Bestiality had been an offence that carried the death penalty since 1533. And in 1828 the law was extended to include both male and female participants when it was held that emission was not necessary for the crime to be committed. It remained a capital offence until 1861 when the Offences against the Person Act reduced the penalty to life imprisonment. Most of the cases involved either dogs, cows or sheep and were lumped together under the general heading of sodomy and buggery.

There appears to have been a rash of bestiality cases brought right at the end of the Georgian period. On 21 August 1834 Cornishman William Hocking, aged fifty-seven, was executed for the crime of bestiality. Several men were convicted of the same offence at Exeter during the 1830s and most of the cases involved young unmarried males with pent-up sexual frustrations. One unusual case involved a man called Goodyer Long, charged with committing bestiality with a female ass in 1837. Goodyer was a married man in his late fifties and was convicted 'on the clearest evidence' at the Lent Assizes in Norfolk on 8 April 1837. Although sentenced to death, the punishment was never carried out. His wife and neighbours lodged a petition calling for leniency and he instead spent some years in rotting prison hulks off the south coast awaiting transportation to Australia. Even that part of the sentence was never carried out. He was eventually released and died in 1853 at the age of seventy-four.

Records in Wales suggest that in the one hundred years from 1730 there were no fewer than twenty-one trials for bestiality. Most involved labourers and servants and in all but one case (which involved an eighteen-year-old servant) the accused was acquitted, generally because it was not possible to prove penetration. Further back in time the Old

Bailey records refer to a 1704 case where, 'Mary Price, alias Hartington of the Parish of Eling, was indicted for the Horrible and abominable Sin of Sodomy committed with a Dog, on the 25th of March last.' She was acquitted after the jury decided that her accuser was 'quarrelsome' and had a history of making complaints against the accused.

Brothel-Keeping

Whereas prostitution was never illegal under Common Law, prosecutions could be brought for 'keeping a bawdy house' if the offence was linked with disorderly conduct, public indecency, or some other crime. This indictable misdemeanour was difficult to establish because of problems in proving who actually owned the premises. Moreover, the sort of evidence needed to prove the offence was generally only available from someone who had actually attended the premises, in other words, as a paying customer. Madams in charge of brothels generally factored in the cost of employing lawyers (to defend them against prosecution) as a business overhead, in effect passing the cost on to their customers.

In the early part of the Georgian period the reform societies pushed for prosecutions to be brought against brothel owners. The records of the Societies for Promoting a Reformation of Manners, in their thirtieth account of the 'Progress made in the Cities of London and Westminster', stated:

> the said Societies have in pursuance of their said design from 1 December 1723 to 1 December 1724 prosecuted divers sorts of offenders viz:
>
> | | |
> |---|---|
> | Lewd and Disorderly Persons | 1951 |
> | Keeping of Bawdy and Disorderly houses | 29 |

They also claimed: 'The total prosecuted in and near London for debauchery and profaneness for the thirty three years past was 89,333.'

In 1752 Parliament passed an Act against the keeping of Disorderly Houses, but this did not in itself criminalise sexual solicitation, e.g. by street walkers. The act was primarily aimed at the public nuisance caused when premises were used for the illegal sale of alcohol, or as gambling dens, or for unlicensed dancing and rowdy entertainment. Unusually, the 1752 act made it a legal requirement that publicly funded prosecutions were to be brought if two or more parishioners were prepared to act as informants. Up until that time, any such prosecutions would have had to have been privately funded. However, few parishioners would volunteer to give evidence that they had entered a brothel, let alone be tarred with the name of 'informer'. The brothel owner was, after all, a neighbour, and generally bawds employed bullies and other 'enforcers' to make sure that complaints from the public never got to court.

What made prosecutions even harder was that a brothel owner had the legal right to transfer the case to the Court of Kings Bench. Doing so meant that the prosecutor lost all chance of recovering legal fees from the Crown. Faced with the expense, few prosecutions were made and as the Society for the Suppression of Vice noted in 1803: 'as the law now stands, the punishment for the offence of keeping a brothel, one of the most heinous and mischievous that can occur in society, is attended with such difficulty as almost entirely to deter from prosecution.'

It was not until the 1818 Disorderly Houses Act was passed that the 'King's Bench escape route' was blocked. It also removed the problem of having to identify the proprietor. The offence was committed by 'any person [...] who shall appear, act or behave him or herself as master or mistress, or as the person having the care, government, or management of any such house.'

Two high-profile cases brought against bawdy-house keepers involved places where sodomy allegedly occurred. One such case was brought against Molly Clap in July 1726, relating to her house in Field Lane, Holborn, and it is dealt with in more detail in the following two chapters. Suffice to say Molly Clap was found guilty. Her defence seemed to consist of arguing that as she was a woman, 'therefore it could not be thought that ever she would be concerned in such abominable practices.' She was sentenced to a spell in the pillory, fined, and sent to prison.

The other case before the Old Bailey, just two years later, involved Julius Caesar Taylor, charged with the dual offences of 'assaulting John Burgess, with an Intent to commit that horrid and detestable Sin of Sodomy and for keeping a disorderly House, and entertaining wicked abandon'd Men, who commit sodomitical Practices.' The court heard that the prisoner was 'seen to sit on the lap of John Burgess, when they committed such indecent and effeminate actions as are not to be mentioned; that the company was referred to his house, launched into such extravagance as was scarce ever heard of.'

The court also heard, 'When any member entered into their society he was christened by a female name and had a quartern of Geneva thrown in his face; one was called Orange Deb, another Nel Guin, and a third Flying Horse Moll and that the prisoner was accessory to these unnatural actions. It likewise appeared by the depositions of several of the neighbours that the prisoner kept a disorderly house and he having none to appear for his character, the jury found him guilty.' The case was part of a number of prosecutions brought against customers found on the premises and the prisoner, Taylor, was fined and required to find sureties for good behaviour.

Retail traders not subject to shop tax, 1787, showing three ladies waiting for custom under the sign of the Turk's Head.

Chapter 11

Where it All Happened: Brothels, Bagnios and Jelly Houses

It would be a mistake to think that paid-for extra-marital sex in the eighteenth century generally involved brothels. This would not have been the norm. In many cases it involved the great outdoors. To the Georgians, our modern world would seem to be obsessed with personal privacy. We not only have indoor flush toilets, we have a room where the toilet is placed, and not only that, but the closet has a door, and a lock. We

The Jelly House Maccaroni, showing a man in elaborate dress embracing a prostitute.

defecate in private, whereas 300 years ago it might be done in the streets, or as Samuel Pepys famously recorded, in the fireplace. Having separate bedrooms – and beds – is considered 'normal' whereas three centuries ago families were much more likely to have shared a bed. Sometimes this extended to total strangers, perhaps using a bolster and/or lying head to toe on the same mattress. Having more than one bed in a room was not unusual, especially in London's crowded housing where personal space was at a premium, and where bed curtains offered the only concession to privacy.

Sex was much more public in the Georgian era. It was frequently performed outdoors, in full view. The diarist James Boswell details many of his pick-ups *en plein aire*, including one on Westminster Bridge. In his words: '10 May, 1763: At the bottom of the Hay-market I picked up a strong jolly young damsel, and taking her under the Arm I conducted her to Westminster-Bridge, and then in armour compleat did I engage her upon this noble Edifice. The whim of doing it there with the Thames rolling below us amused me much. Yet after the brutish appetite was sated I could not but despise myself for being so closely united with such a low Wretch.'

The 'armour' was a condom, and the sexual encounter must have been witnessed by dozens of people. On another occasion (25 March 1763) Boswell writes: 'As I was coming home this night I felt carnal inclinations raging thro' my frame. I determined to gratify them. I went to St. James's Park and […] picked up a Whore. For the first time did I engage in Armour which I found but a dull satisfaction. She who submitted to my lusty embraces was a young Shropshire girl only seventeen, very well-looked, her name Elizabeth Parker.'

Six days later the lustful Boswell wrote: 'At night I strolled into the Park and took the first Whore I met, whom I without many words copulated with free from danger, being safely sheeth'd. She was ugly and lean and her breath smelt of spirits. I never asked her name.'

Going to Ranelagh Gardens, or, better still, Vauxhall Gardens, a visitor would find quiet alleys and dark corners which were positively swarming with amorous couples. And these are just the well-known public gardens: there were an estimated sixty-five public open spaces in London in the 1700s; typically, fields attached to taverns and used as tea gardens or by people taking the waters from local springs. All doubled up as places favoured for sexual encounters. Bluntly, fornication was there for all to see.

This was especially true at the lower end of the scale. The so called 'threepenny stand-ups' – a quick fumble in a shop doorway – was all that was needed. Next up the scale would have been the whore with the use of a garret room, say, in one of the hugely overcrowded wards such as St Giles. The image of *The Last Shift* by James Gillray (see Plate 2) gives an idea of the joyless, drab setting. Then there would have been the bagnios: originally a site of public baths but by the Georgian era often a euphemism for a whore house. The girls would not have lived in, so in that sense it was not a brothel. A couple could rent a room by the hour, and the proprietor would provide basic services, sometimes including light food and alcohol. Similarly, many taverns would have rooms which could be rented out on a short-term basis. Here, a man could pick-up a girl in the bar and go upstairs. Alternatively, as described by Casanova on page 21 the host would be able to provide a 'beauty parade' of females so that the male customer could make his selection.

A popular landlord would no doubt have a list of girls he could call on, either to come to his tavern (just send a link boy to fetch her) or he would have a list of recommendations and addresses which he could hand to punters. From this grew the idea of a printed directory of local sex workers, such as *Harris's List*, published between 1757 and 1795. It was never intended to be comprehensive or exhaustive, and it related to just a small area around Covent Garden, the epicentre of the sex trade. Edinburgh had its own directory, and other cities may have had handwritten lists, although in an age of low literacy it was much more likely that the knowledge – the 'who, where, what and how much' – would have been passed on by the local publican by word of mouth.

These lists were kept by publicans who were happy to act as pimp, and each would have his own list. In 1771 Richard King had published a book under the title of *The New London Spy, or, a Twenty-four hour ramble through the Bills of Mortality*. It promised readers a 'true picture of modern high and low life, from the splendid mansions of St James's to the subterranean habitations of St Giles's, wherein are displayed the various scenes of Covent Garden and its environs, the theatres, the jelly houses [...] night houses [...] and other places of entertainments.' It particularly draws the reader's attention to a 'smart fellow at the door of M.l.t.by's bagnio, revising a paper. It contains a list of what dainty bits he can furnish his lascivious customers with in the flesh way, so that this roll may be considered as his bill of fare, describing the size, complexion, quality and price of the commodities in which he deals. That is one of the most eminent fleshmongers in the whole circle of this chaste spot, and is applied to the first ladies of pleasure in his extensive town, who deem it highly honourable, as well as advantageous, to be inserted in this list.'

King's book mentions the jelly houses: places where initial encounters would take place. The image which appears on page 116 shows a well-dressed man, in this case known as a macaroni, in a jelly house where he is shown embracing a prostitute he has picked up. The jelly house was not in itself a 'knocking shop' but it was a place to meet, share a drink and perhaps order a light meal, such as a delicately-flavoured aphrodisiac like a jelly, and then move on to a bagnio or rooms for hire.

The London and Westminster Guide of 1766 informed its readers that: 'Covent Garden is the great square of Venus, and its purlieus are crowded with the votaries of this goddess. One would imagine that all the prostitutes in the kingdom had pitched upon this pleasant neighbourhood for a place of general rendezvous. For here are lewd women in sufficient numbers to people a mighty colony.' It went on to say: 'The jelly houses are now become the resort of abandoned rakes and shameless prostitutes. These and the taverns afford an ample supply of provisions for the flesh, while others abound for the consummation of the desires which are thus excited.'

In the area around Drury Lane a favourite meeting place was Moll King's Coffee House, run by husband-and-wife Tom and Molly King from 1722. When Tom died, Molly took over the business until she retired in 1745, successfully resisting any charge of running a brothel because sex was not actually taking place in or above the coffee shop. People would meet up, agree terms, and head off for a nearby bagnio or else find a suitable alleyway near the play houses of Covent Garden. Some of the prostitutes made the transition from whore to madam, one case being Betty Carless (she generally adopted the name Careless, to show her carefree nature). Famous as a whore in the 1720s, when her looks faded she moved on to being a bawd at a house in the Little Piazza at Covent Garden, before ending up dying, penniless, in 1739.

Her old home in Little Piazza, on the corner of Russell Street, was acquired by Jane Douglas, otherwise known as Mother Douglas or the Empress of Bawds. She decorated the place to the highest standard, and employed liveried servants to wait upon her male guests, who were happy to pay handsomely for the chance to relax in opulent surroundings and to be presented with the chance to meet and negotiate terms with a steady stream of young actresses, flower girls or 'flash mollishers'. After a few years Mother Douglas took over larger and even more prestigious premises – the former Kings Head tavern – and added a restaurant to entertain her customers. These included various members of the royal family. Prince William, Duke of Cumberland, was a regular visitor for a time and the place proved to be particularly popular with wealthy members of the East India Company, including Robert Clive, who went on to become the Commander-in-Chief of British India.

But, in time, the rich and famous stopped visiting, and as the clientele moved downmarket, profits slumped and Mother Douglas became ill. She was described as 'much bloated by Drink and Debauch [...] her Legs swelled out of shape [...] suffering great discomfort,' and died on 10 June 1761, leaving a sizeable estate.

A description of a Covent Garden bagnio was given by Casanova following his visit to London in 1763 as being a place where 'a rich man can sup, bathe and sleep with a fashionable courtesan of which species there are many in London. It makes a magnificent debauch, and only costs six guineas.' The German writer Archenholz went into more detail, writing: 'In London there is a certain kind of house, called bagnios, which are supposed to be baths; their real purpose, however, is to provide persons of both sexes with pleasure. These houses are well and often richly furnished and every device for exciting the senses is either at hand or can be provided. Girls do not live here, but they are fetched in sedan chairs when required [...] All noise and uproar is banned here, no loud footsteps are heard, every corner is carpeted and the numerous attendants speak quietly amongst themselves.'

Oddly, not all bagnios were dens of immorality. Perhaps in the same way that nowadays it is possible to expect a massage in some massage parlours, so, in the eighteenth century it was still possible to visit a bagnio and expect to be able to enjoy a bath. The Hummums and Lovejoy's in Covent Garden were cases in point. But these 'respectable' bagnios were the exception to the rule. One particularly well-known bagnio was the Turk's Head, in Bow Street, Covent Garden. Run by a Mrs Earl, it features in Plate V of William Hogarth's series of six satirical plates entitled *Marriage a la mode* (and is shown on page 5 in the plate section). The image gives an idea of the somewhat shabby interior of the room, where the husband is shown in his death throes after being stabbed by his wife's lover, who exits smartly via the window. The same bagnio features prominently on page 115 showing three ladies of what was called the Cyprian Corps, standing in the doorway under the sign of the Turk's Head, ready to entice passing males to come inside. Mind you, a wise visitor would have learned from *Harris's List* that it was advisable to avoid the 'contaminated carcase' of Miss Young. In its 1779 edition readers of the List were warned:

> Miss Young, No. 6, Cumberland Court or Turk's Head Bagnio, Bridge's Street. Miss Young is an adopted child to the bawd, who keeps, or more properly speaking, is kept by the above mentioned houses, and is so very fond of cutting a figure, that in a hired tawdry silk gown, she will fancy herself a woman of the first quality. We mentioned her in the last list as tolerably handsome, but of a disposition mercenary, almost beyond example, her beauty is now vanished, but her avarice remains, and what is worse, she has very lately had the folly and wickedness to leave a certain hospital, before the cure of a certain distemper which she had was completed, and has thrown her contaminated carcase on the town again, for which we hold her inexcusable, and which was our only reason for repeating her name, that her company might be avoided, and that she might be held in the infamous light she so justly deserves for her wilful villainy.

The Turk's Head was clearly a popular rendezvous for women with 'loose morals' and features in the proceedings of the House of Lords when, in

1790, William Raybould petitioned for a divorce from his wife. Thomas Kirk was called to give evidence, with the report stating that he knew Mrs Raybould because he frequently passed by the door to the room she was in when he was a waiter at the Turk's Head. '[She] came several times to the hotel with Gentlemen.' Being asked if she stayed all night with them, he replied, 'Sometimes she did, sometimes she did not,' and in answer to the question about whether the gentlemen slept with Mrs Raybould, Kirk replied that 'he could not say whether they slept, but they were in bed together.' He also reported that she visited once or twice a week, for several months. Being asked if he knew the gentlemen who came with her, he replied: 'No, so many were coming in and out it was impossible to identify anyone.' Later Kirk was cross-examined as to how he knew that the couple were in bed together. His reply, 'By opening the door to give an answer to anything they called for.' On being asked if 'he did go into the room and see them in bed together?' he responded', Yes, frequently.' The evidence, and a report from a Dr Hall that he had treated Mrs Raybould for venereal disease, was sufficient for their Lordships to give the Private Bill a second reading and it was passed back to the House of Commons. It was one of comparatively few Divorce Bills brought before Parliament.

What is clear from all the descriptions of the time is that finding a prostitute was never a problem. Popular meeting places such as Bagnigge Wells (near Camden) as well as public open spaces such as Ranelagh and Vauxhall were teeming with women offering their services. The more upmarket ladies would no doubt have rooms nearby. And, just as in today's red-light district in Amsterdam, ladies would sit at open windows enticing in passers-by.

There were of course brothels, usually where prostitutes either lived in, or were called in as and when required. Run by a madam who would often provide fine silks and embroidered clothing to the girls in her charge, at exorbitant rates of interest, these brothels covered the entire spectrum of class and decorum. At the top end were establishments such as those run by Charlotte Hayes in King's Place, off Pall Mall, which attracted the custom of upper-class gentlemen. Charlotte was perhaps the most successful of all the brothel-keepers, starting off in Soho in Berwick Street and Great Marlborough Street, and then opening premises in St James's, at King's Place and in Arlington Street. She spent extravagantly and was committed to debtors' prisons on several occasions, but ended up living with an Irish gambler and racehorse-owner called Dennis O'Kelly. He owned a magnificent stallion called Eclipse, unbeaten on the track, and a horse which could command a fortune at stud. Together, O'Kelly and Hayes amassed a fortune estimated at £70,000; equivalent today to rather more than five million pounds.

Another famous brothel-owner in London was Elizabeth Needham, otherwise known as Mother Needham. She was shown as the procuress and brothel-keeper greeting the innocent young maid Moll Hackabout in the first plate of William Hogarth's series of satirical etchings, *A Harlot's Progress*. She kept what was described as a 'notorious disorderly house' in Park Place, near London's St James's Street, and was believed to have acted as a procuress for the loathsome Colonel Charteris, mentioned already on page 102. Another famous bawd was Mother Wisebourne, whose house in Covent Garden was one of the most expensive brothels in the first few decades of the Georgian period. One of her girls was Sarah Pridden, better known as Sally Salisbury. The jewel in Mother Wisebourne's crown, and the first of the century's true celebrity whores, Pridden joined Mother Needham when Mother Wisebourne died, but, as described at page 36, ended up dying in prison after wounding her lover in a knife attack.

Brothels were often the scene of petty crimes, especially thefts from clients. They were also frequently the source of outbreaks of violence, one of the most famous occurring on 1 July 1749. Three sailors from *The Grafton* had visited a brothel in The Strand and had their possessions stolen, including their watches and a considerable quantity of money. They vowed revenge, and headed for Wapping to get reinforcements. They returned later that night with forty sailors and thoroughly trashed the brothel, setting it on fire. They were careful not to steal any items. They simply destroyed the prostitutes' furniture and belongings. The sailors returned over the following nights to continue their crusade against neighbouring bawdy-houses, bringing with them a number of enthusiastic drunken followers. One of these was the unfortunate Bosavern Penlez, a young apprentice who had spent most of the day getting thoroughly inebriated. Encountering the rioters, he seized upon the confusion to help himself to a bundle of linen from the house of one Peter Wood. Penlez was caught, tried and hanged at Tyburn in October 1749, even though he was not one of the main architects of the rioting.

Brothels were always to be found in the areas of London where housing was cheap and overcrowded, such as the dockland area to the east of the city, with its high population of sailors. During the previous century what was known as the Ratcliffe Highway – the area lying immediately to the north of the waterfront at Wapping – became notorious for its brothels catering to the needs of returning sailors. Britain's merchant navy tripled in size during the eighteenth century, and the demand for prostitutes similarly multiplied. For that reason, all the major port cities had flourishing sex trades, particularly Bristol, Plymouth and Portsmouth. In London, the area of St Giles, situated on the road between Holborn and Tyburn, had originally been a small village, but numbers swelled throughout the Georgian era so that by 1830 some 30,000 people were living in the parish, often with as many as fifty inhabitants to a four-bedroom property. St Giles became notorious as a centre for lower-class brothels, and had perhaps the worst slums to be found anywhere in London.

To end with: two instances which act as a reminder that men were forever looking for new and exciting places where they could indulge their sexual fantasies. The first involves Brooks' Club. It still has a record of the bet made in 1785 by Lord Cholmondeley with Lord Derby to the effect that Lord Cholmondeley would join what would now be termed the Mile-High Club. No sooner had the balloon craze got under way than these two aristocrats were wagering that Lord Cholmondeley would have his wicked way with 'Mrs E...t' in the basket of a hot air balloon. There is no record of how close the randy lord got to winning his bet, or what 'Mrs E...t' thought of the idea. She was Grace Dalrymple Elliott, with whom his lordship had a lengthy affair. The wager demonstrates the

Where it All Happened: Brothels, Bagnios and Jelly Houses 125

very open nature of such conquests, as well as showing the popularity of ever more adventurous and obscure places where sex might take place. The second example is a drawing made by Thomas Rowlandson entitled 'Love on two wheels'. It shows a couple copulating, while balanced on a platform supported by two wheels. No matter that the bicycle had not yet been invented: men were already working out ways of using it for sexual purposes!

An evening's invitation; with a wink from the Bagnio, showing two prostitutes picking the pocket of a client, while the brothel's madam looks on. A link-boy lights the way.

Chapter 12

Sodomites

Homosexuality (generally referred to in the Georgian era as sodomy) deserves to be looked at in a completely separate chapter from lesbian behaviour – and cross-dressing – because lesbianism (generally known as sapphism) was never illegal. Cross-dressing was not only legal but had its place in public entertainment, at masquerades, for example, and the only time it crossed the line into illegality was where it was used to deceive and thereby gain financial

Edward Rigby, convicted of attempted sodomy, striking an unrepentant pose in 1703.

advantage. Sodomy on the other hand was always illegal and carried the heaviest of penalties.

That is not to say that the general public universally condemned sodomy, although it is fair to say that if a man was put in the pillory for sodomitical acts, his most violent assailants, hurling rotten vegetables, offal and rubbish, were likely to be women, especially prostitutes, who detested sodomites. In general though, across the board, the public were more willing to turn a blind eye to same-sex love, even if the law and the church continued to be vehemently opposed. By the middle of the century an obscure British writer called Thomas Cannon issued a pamphlet entitled *Ancient and Modern Pederasty Investigated and Exemplify'd*. It is described as the first public defence of homosexual acts. Pederasty is the sexual relationship between an adult male and an adolescent male, and is a term particularly used to refer to historical practices in Ancient Greece and Ancient Rome.

Writing in 1749, Cannon described:

> That celebrated passion, sealed by sensualists, espoused by philosophers, enshrined by kings, [which] is now exploded with one accord and disowned by the meanest beggar. Wherefore since fashion discountenances, law punishes, God forbids, the detested Love, we may sure discuss it with freedom and the most philosophical exactness. Every dabbler knows by his classics that it was pursued and praised with the height of liberty, boy love ever was the top refinement of most enlightened ages. Unnatural Desire is a Contradiction in Terms; downright Nonsense. Desire is an amatory Impulse of the inmost human Parts: Are not they, however constructed, and consequently impelling, Nature? Nature sometimes assumes an unusual appearance, but the extraordinary pederast seeing fruition is as naturally acted as the ordinary woman's man in that pursuit.

Pederasty lurked in the dark streets of London on moonless nights, with link-boys sharing a dubious reputation as child prostitutes. They were employed to guide late-night travellers to their homes, carrying a link, i.e. flaming torch, in front to light the road. But they became synonymous with despicable, dishonest or perverted behaviour. In 1771 Sir Joshua Reynolds painted a dark picture entitled *Cupid as a Link Boy*. It shows a dishevelled young link boy as a cupid, but a cupid with a difference. This cupid did not sport the white wings of an angel, but black bat wings. He holds his link in an obviously phallic manner. The message is unmistakable: the link boys were figures of immorality, willing to lead men astray. They also had a reputation for dishonesty and thieving, as John Gay warned in his *Trivia* in 1716:

> Let constant Vigilance thy Footsteps guide;
> And wary Circumspection guard thy side;
> Then shalt thou walk unharm'd the dang'rous Night,
> Nor need th'officious Link-Boy's smoky Light.

Before looking at the 'gay scene' in the eighteenth century it helps to unlearn some of the things we take for granted. Nowadays we often see pressure being brought for people to 'come out' and even moves to 'out' those who refuse. We are used to speculation that if a man has no female partner, and chooses to spend his time in the company of other men, that he may be homosexual. And above all, we assume that sex is the basis of all really close non-family relationships. Contrast this with the situation 300 years ago. There was no question of people choosing to come out: to do so would be to admit to being a sodomite, an offence which was so abhorrent in the eyes of the law that it carried the death penalty. To find an equivalent to the horror felt by authorities in the Georgian era, you would have to compare it with bestiality with your neighbour's pet Labrador: it carried that sort of opprobrium.

Of course, there were attempts to 'out' men suspected of homosexual tendencies, often linked to attempted extortion and blackmail. For some, such as the mentally unstable Lord Castlereagh, foreign secretary during the Regency period, the fear of being outed was enough to drive him to commit suicide in 1822.

For others, fear of being charged with what was always described as either an 'unnatural crime' or an 'abhorrent crime' led them to flee the country. Take William Courtenay, later to become the 9th Earl of Devon. Known as 'Kitty, he was brought up in a predominately female world, with thirteen sisters and no brothers. As a youngster he was befriended by the art collector William Beckford. Throughout his teens he had a homosexual affair with Beckford, who was eight years his senior. Finally, news of the affair, and of letters which had been intercepted between the pair, came to the attention of Lord Loughborough. He was William's uncle and he went on to become Lord High Chancellor of Great Britain from 1793 to 1801. Wishing to see William disgraced, for his own dynastic reasons, the uncle decided that news of the affair should be released to the press. Knowing that being hauled before the court in Exeter could lead to humiliation – if not a death sentence – William Courtenay packed his bags and left England, settling first in New York and later in France. Clearly, both the Americans and the French were more broad-minded than the English about such things.

We tend to question the sexuality of any prominent male in public office who is not married, but back in the 1700s there were countless cases where men preferred male company, but were nevertheless free from criticism or judgment. William Pitt the Younger is a case in point. Made prime minister at the age of twenty-four, it appears that he was fond of the company of men, especially Bob Steele, the Secretary to the Treasury. They were known to spend time together, and stayed at Brighton, but whether theirs was a sexual relationship was not known. Certainly, the *Morning Post* was sufficiently bold to write slyly about Pitt's lack of knowledge of women:

> Tis true, indeed, we oft abuse him,
> Because he bends to no man;
> But slander's self dares not accuse him
> Of stiffness to a woman.

All we know is that the young Pitt never felt confident with women and although at one stage he appeared to have 'an understanding' with Eleanor Eden, he backed off from the relationship, stating in a letter to the girl's father, 'I am compelled to say that I find the obstacles to it decisive and insurmountable.' Of course, the decisive and insurmountable obstacle may have been sexual, although one suspects that acute shyness, coupled with a lack of emotional maturity, may have contributed.

Another man with a reputation for asexuality was Horace Walpole. Our modern preoccupation with establishing a person's sexuality has led some to argue that Horace Walpole had a sexual relationship with Henry Pelham-Clinton (at that stage the 9th Earl of Lincoln) while he was a young man visiting Italy on his Grand Tour. The couple then quarrelled and the earl married his cousin, Catherine Pelham, whereas Walpole never married.

There is no suggestion that any of Walpole's subsequent romantic interludes with females were ever consummated, and his contemporaries often joked about his effeminate behaviour, one calling him 'a hermaphrodite horse'. His mannerisms – especially his habit of walking into a room on tiptoes as if he were a woman wearing heels – caught the notice of many. His circle of friends included men who were suspected of being homosexual. Samuel Johnson's friend, Hester Thrale, was convinced that she could tell a sodomite just by looking at how he moved his hands, and as far as she was concerned Walpole's friend and pen-pal, Sir Horace Mann, was a 'finger twirler'. In the mind of Hester Thrale finger twirling was an absolute giveaway, and she writes in her diary: 'Mrs Greatheed & I call those Fellows Finger-twirlers; – meaning a decent word for Sodomites.' She was convinced that cold weather had something to do with making men fancy other men, writing: 'The Scotch seem strangely addicted to this Enormity, & 'tis a cold Country too: – I can think of no Reason but one – their wearing Fillibegs [fillibeg is another word for a kilt].'

In all probability Walpole simply suppressed his homosexuality, and this may have had much to do with the effect of watching his elder brother, Edward, being charged with homosexuality after he was alleged to have attempted to sodomize an eighteen-year-old Irish boy who had applied for a job in Sir Edward's household. Horace Walpole gave evidence in support of his brother, and would have seen at first-hand how the allegation of sodomy threatened to destroy everything the family had acquired. There may or may not have been a blackmail plot behind the allegations of sodomy, but the whole episode would have convinced Horace that adopting a life of complete celibacy was simply the only option.

Branding aesthetes like Walpole as 'closet homosexuals', after the event, is complicated by the fact that many of the affected mannerisms (think limp wrists and mincing walk) were deliberately adopted in the eighteenth century as a sign of how cultured a person was. The Grand Tour had a lot to answer for, leading to the fashion for 'macaronis' to strut their stuff in the 1760s and '70s. Nowadays we would see such dress and mannerisms as indicating effeminacy, whereas 250 years ago it was more likely to give rise to an insulting cry of 'French dog' if a man was encountered in the street while dressed in macaroni style, with tight jackets and high, powdered, wigs. The *Oxford Magazine* in 1770 had described the macaroni as, 'a kind of animal, neither male nor female, a thing of the neuter gender, lately started up among us. It is called a macaroni. It talks without meaning, it smiles without pleasantry, it eats without appetite, it rides without exercise, it wenches without passion.'

The point is: fashion did not necessarily tell us much about underlying sexuality. Some homosexuals may have dressed *a la macaroni*. Some aristocrats may have returned from Italy after their Grand Tour having sampled homosexual pleasures. But equally, there were always devoted followers of fashion who simply wanted to ape their social superiors and would not have seen their appearance or behaviour as indicating homosexual leanings. But when you look at the macaronis in context of the popularity for cross-dressing at masquerades, it shows that British society was fascinated with the whole question of sexual behaviour, appearances, and the freedom to explore self-expression.

The church authorities were outraged, with the Bishop of London leading the opposition to masquerades where cross-dressing was prevalent. It would be a mistake to think that puritanism and religious bigotry had disappeared with the Restoration of the Monarchy: it had not, and remained as an important undercurrent, resurfacing throughout the century. For instance the Society for the Reformation of Manners – or 'SRM' and for 'manners' read 'moral behaviour' – had been founded in the 1690s with the avowed purpose of cleaning up the city, taking a swipe at profane swearing and cursing, Sabbath breaking, drunkenness, lewd and disorderly conduct, brothel-keeping, gaming, and sodomy.

The SRM branched out into at least twenty other cities across the country, but in London one of its first acts was to try to nail Edward

Rigby, master of the naval ship *Dragon*. He had been acquitted before a court martial of sodomising a sailor, but his unrepentant behaviour made him a target for the SRM. Rigby was lured into inviting a servant called William Minton into a private room at the George Tavern in Pall Mall. Ensconced in the adjoining room were a constable, two assistants and a clerk to the court. Down came the trousers and in rushed the zealous reformers. Rigby could not be charged with sodomy because this required the dual proof of both penetration and, most importantly, ejaculation. He was therefore charged with attempted sodomy. He was convicted, fined £1,000, sent to the stocks for three days, and jailed for a year. The engraving of him appearing on page 126 was made in 1703, and shows the defiant Captain Rigby shortly before he decided to join the navy of England's main rival, France.

The SRM had started in the Tower Hamlets area of London with the aid of paid informants. It engineered prosecutions against playwrights for writing immoral and lewd works; it brought charges against brothel owners; and it sought to stamp out all homosexual behaviour, seen as 'an evil force invading our land'.

In 1707 a ballad sheet was published commemorating the story of how some forty men were rounded up in an informal club near the Royal Exchange and thrown in gaol at the Comptor. Three committed suicide while awaiting trial. The arrests led to successful prosecutions of at least eight men, reported in a paper entitled '*The Tryal and Conviction of several Reputed Sodomites, before the Right Honourable the Lord Mayor, and Recorder of London, at Guild-Hall, the 20th Day of October, 1707*'. The writer Rictor Norton gives details of the case, and of many other trials, in his online publication, *Homosexuality in Eighteenth-Century England: A Sourcebook*. The considerable publicity generated by the trials, and in particular the newspaper reports giving detailed accounts of sodomy and mutual masturbation, led Daniel Defoe to call for trials to be held away from the public gaze (he said that this was the Dutch preference). He felt that reporting such trials was wrong and in his *A Review of the State of the British Nation* Defoe concluded that reporting homosexual activities was 'both offensive to the Ears of the Virtuous, and serves but to excite and gratify the corrupted Appetites of the Vicious.'

The SRM was unrelenting in its pursuit of men who frequented molly-houses (taverns where homosexuals, known as mollies, were known to meet). As early as 1709 the journalist Ned Ward published *The Secret History of the London Clubs* and although he may have embroidered some of the details, his commentary about Molly Clubs, the mimicking of women and the re-enactment of giving birth, give an insight into the rituals and role-play practised by the mollies:

> THERE are a particular Gang of Wretches in Town, who call themselves Mollies, & are so far degenerated from all Masculine Deportment or Manly exercises that they rather fancy themselves as Women, imitating all the little Vanities that Custom has reconcil'd to the Female sex, affecting to speak, walk, tattle, curtsy, cry, scold, & mimick all manner of Effeminacy. At a certain Tavern in the City, whose sign I shall not mention, because I am unwilling to fix an Odium on the House, they have a settled & constant Meeting. When they are met, together, their usual Practice is to mimick a female Gossiping & fall into all the impertinent Tittle Tattle that a merry Society of good Wives can be subject to. Not long since they had cushioned up one of their Brethren, or rather Sisters, according to Female Dialect, disguising him in a Woman's Night-Gown, Sarsanet Hood, & Night-rail who when the Company were men, was to mimick a woman, produce a jointed Baby they had provided, which wooden Offspring was to be after-wards Christened, whilst one in a High Crown'd Hat, I am old Beldam's Pinner, representing[ed] a Country Midwife, & another dizen'd up in a Huswife's Coif for a Nurse & all the rest of an impertinent Decorum of a Christening.
>
> And for the further promotion of their unbecoming mirth, every one was to talk of their Husbands & Children, one extolling the Virtues of her Husband, another the genius & wit of their Children; whilst a Third would express himself sorrowfully under the character of a Widow.
>
> Thus every one in his turn makes scoff of the little Effeminacy & Weaknesses, which Women are subject to, when gossiping o'er their cups on purpose to extinguish that Natural Affection which is due to the Fair Sex & to turn their Juvenile desires towards preter-

natural polotions. They continued their practices till they were happily routed by the conduct of some of the under Agents to the Reforming Society, so that several of them were brought to open Punishment, which happily put a Period to their Scandalous Revels.

Other reports, in particular contained in accounts of trials for sodomy, echo this transvestite role-playing, particularly with mock marriages and mock trials.

There were a series of raids on molly-houses in 1725 culminating in the raid in February 1726 on Margaret Clap's coffee house in Holborn. The enterprising Mother Clap had opened her house to the public as a coffee house in 1724 but it quickly became a meeting place for homosexuals. The raid followed many months of surveillance, backed up by information obtained from disaffected mollies and paid informants. The Old Bailey reports of the trial, available online, quote one Samuel Stevens as saying: 'On Sunday Night the 14th of November. I went to the Prisoners House in Field-Lane, Holbourn. I found near Men Fifty there, making Love to one another as they call'd it. Sometimes they'd sit in one anothers Laps, use their Hands indecently, Dance and make Curtsies and mimick the Language of Women [...] Then they would hug, and play, and toy, and go out by couples into another room on the same floor to be married, as they called it.'

Margaret Clap was convicted of keeping a disorderly house for the entertainment of sodomites. She was fined, sent to be pilloried at Smithfield, and sentenced to two years in prison. In practice she is believed to have died before the year was out. As a result of the raid, a number of prosecutions were brought, leading to the execution of three men. Most of the men charged were set free due to lack of evidence, but a number were fined, pilloried and sent to prison.

On another occasion, in 1726, Thomas Wright was indicted for committing buggery with Thomas Newton. Newton gave evidence that the accused: 'had the Carnal Use of my Body at his own House, in Christophers Alley in Moor-fields.'

A group of homosexuals had quarrelled, and the evidence from one of them helped paint a picture of an assembly where there were: '8 or 9 [men] in a large Room, one was playing upon a Fiddle, and others were [...] dancing in obscene Postures, and others while Singing baudy Songs, and talking leudly, and Acting a great many Indecencies.' Wright was executed on 6 May 1726 at Tyburn. A whole raft of prosecutions was brought against molly-house proprietors and their customers throughout the 1720s. *Mist's Weekly Journal* of 7 May 1726 contained the following report:

> We hear that near 20 Houses have been discover'd, which entertain'd Sodomitical Clubs; besides the nocturnal Assemblies of great Numbers of the like vile Persons at what they call the Markets, which are the Royal-Exchange, Moorfields, Lincolns-Inn Bog-houses, the South Side of St. James's Park and the Piazza's of Covent-Garden, where they make their Bargains, and then withdraw into some dark Corners to indorse, as they call it, but in plain English to commit Sodomy. However the Government having undertaken the Prosecution of them, 'tis not doubted, but strict Care will be taken to detect them in order to avert from these Cities those just Judgments, which fell from Heaven upon Sodom and Gomorrah.

Mother Clap's may have been a particularly well-known molly house but others enjoyed great popularity, including Plump Nelly's in Giltspur Street, run by Samuel Roper (otherwise known as 'Plump Nelly'). He was charged with sodomy and also for keeping a disorderly house, but died in the local prison while awaiting trial. Another was in Tottenham Court Road, run by someone who was in all probability an African, going by the splendid name of Julius Caesar Taylor. His trial has already been mentioned in Chapter 10. Taylor, and a man called John Burgess, were jointly charged with sodomy and evidence was heard that they committed, 'filthy lewd actions which will not bear mentioning to a modest ear, that they appeared equally pleas'd, Julius Caesar Taylor using indecent Gestures and Burgess suffering them.'

Generally, the lack of corroborating evidence from third-party witnesses meant that the suspects were often charged not with sodomy, but with the lesser offence of 'assault with intent'. Hence in December 1730 a case was brought against two men, William Hollywell and William Huggins. Hollywell was indicted 'for an Assault, with an Intent to commit the detestable Crime of Buggery', while Huggins was charged with 'consenting and submitting to the same'. The case arose when the two men were caught in the act of having anal sex on the stairwell in St Paul's Cathedral. Hollywell ran off, but when he was apprehended his shirt was examined. On it 'appear'd plain Tokens of Emission' and both of the men were found guilty. In the case of William Hollywell, he was sentenced 'to stand on the Pillory near St. Paul's, for an Hour, to suffer 6 Months Imprisonment, and to pay a Fine of £40.'

William Huggins, the consenting party, was ordered 'to stand on the Pillory for an Hour at the same Place, and to suffer Eight Months Imprisonment'. Being pilloried was no easy punishment: offal, small stones, excrement and rotten vegetables would be hurled at the men from close quarters, often resulting in serious head injuries and sometimes death.

A case which came to trial in 1772 highlighted, in the minds of the public, the link between effeminate dress (macaroni style) and homosexual behaviour. It involved Captain Jones, accused of sodomising a thirteen-year old boy. An analysis of the case and its wider implications appears in Appendix 1.

The SRM resurfaced in various forms throughout the century. In 1756 a group of Dissenters, Methodist ministers and magistrates led by John Fielding started a push against Sabbath-breaking and brothel keeping, with John Wesley claiming that within six years they had brought nearly 10,000 prosecutions and that in a seven-month period from August 1762 nearly 1,000 people had been brought to trial (550 for lewdness and keeping a brothel, 400 for Sabbath-breaking, and forty for gaming and profane swearing). But the public were increasingly alarmed at the reliance upon paid informants and over-zealous constables. A further tide of prosecutions followed after the formation of the Proclamation Society in 1789. Launched by King George III at the instigation of reformer William Wilberforce it took aim at 'dissolute immoral or disorderly practices'.

But if paid informers, blackmailers and meddling politicians were a threat to men suspected of homosexual behaviour, they also had to contend with scorned or aggrieved third parties. Chapter 10 includes the story of the bigamist Elizabeth Chudleigh, Duchess of Kingston.

The actor-playwright Samuel Foote had tried to put on a play called *A Trip to Calais*, in which the thinly disguised figure of the duchess was represented by a coarse, avaricious woman named Kitty Crocodile. Foote's purpose may have been no more than to extort money from Elizabeth: he reportedly turned up at her house and read aloud passages to the mortified lady, and demanded £2,000 in return for agreeing not to have the play published. By all accounts Elizabeth tried to outflank Foote by using her influence with the Lord Chamberlain, who was happy to have the play banned. Outraged, Foote took the story to the papers. Matters were made worse when Elizabeth responded to a letter written by Foote, and he simply published the exchange of letters, which brought the entire saga out into the open.

Within days of the trial, in which the Duchess was found guilty of bigamy, pamphlets giving lurid details of events appeared not just in London but across the country, but the Duchess was not about to forget or forgive Samuel Foote. She employed the Reverend William Jackson as her secretary. He wrote articles in the 'Public Ledger' suggesting that Foote was a homosexual. Foote successfully sued for libel, but the Reverend, probably bankrolled by Elizabeth, and using the *nom de plume* of Humphrey Nettle, published a lengthy attack on Foote under the title of 'Sodom and Onan.' It contained a recognisable portrait of Foote, together with an illustration of a large naked foot. The satire attacked Foote as a sodomite, and Foote responded by re-writing *A Trip to Calais* as *The Capuchin*, with Reverend William Jackson lampooned as 'Dr Viper'. The attacks became more and more personal and the German writer Archenholz wrote that: 'A criminal prosecution was commenced, on a charge [of sodomy] against Foote, the celebrated comedian, about a year before his death. The intrepid actor soon after appeared upon the stage [...] But the noise from the pit, and the epithet made use of, and repeated from box to box, entirely disconcerted him. At length he obtained liberty to speak. He then assured the audience that he was innocent, and besought them not to condemn him unheard.'

In practice, criminal charges had been brought against Foote in late 1776. He appeared before the King's Bench to answer the allegation, made by his former footman, John Sangster, that Foote had 'attempted to commit an unnatural act upon his person' twice in May 1775. Lord

Mansfield heard the case, and concluded that the whole thing was a conspiracy to blacken Foote's character, and Foote was acquitted. But the damage had been done, and Foote died, a broken man, shortly afterwards. He was fifty-seven.

Did the general public care about homosexuality? Well, possibly they simply accepted the view of Archenholz, writing in *A Picture of England*, where he says:

> The English women are so handsome, and the desire to please them, and to obtain their favours, is so ardent and so general that it is not in the least surprizing that those islanders should hold a certain unnatural crime in the utmost abhorrence. They speak in no part of the world with so much horror of this infamous passion, as in England. The punishment by law is imprisonment, and the pillory. With this accusation, it is however better to suffer death at once, for, on such an occasion, the fury of the populace is unbounded, and even the better sort of people have no compassion for the culprit.

Archenholz went on to explain convictions for sodomy were rare, 'not on account of the paucity of the numbers charged [...] but because they never yield to such a brutal appetite but with the utmost precaution.' In other words, men made absolutely sure that there was not a remotest chance of getting 'caught in the act'.

What all of this shows is that there was undoubtedly a 'gay scene' in cities such as London, but it was low-key to the point of being largely hidden from public view. There were exceptions, and the road linking Upper and Middle Moorfields, London, (today forming the south side of Finsbury Square) was known throughout the eighteenth century as the Sodomite's Walk. Sections of St James's Park and Lincoln's Inn Fields had a similar reputation. But in general, because the law remained implacably opposed to sodomy throughout the Georgian era, homosexuals lived their lives in fear of being caught, betrayed or blackmailed. A detailed look at one particular case, involving life on board the Royal Navy ship the *Africaine*, appears in Appendix 1. The last case where sodomites were hanged at Newgate was on 27 November 1835, right at the end of the Georgian era. The prisoners were John Smith and James (sometimes referred to as John) Pratt and they were both executed for what the Old Bailey trial records describe as having 'feloniously, wickedly, diabolically, and against the order of nature, carnally [...] commit[ted] and perpetrate[d] the detestable, horrid, and abominable crime (among Christians not to be named) called buggery.' The men had been visited in their final days by a young Charles Dickens, who wrote about his visit in his essay *A visit to Newgate*, later to become part of *Sketches by Boz*.

The Woman Haters Lamentation, showing (L to R) a double suicide scene with one man hanging from a noose, while another stabs himself; two gays caressing and dancing; a woman cuts down the body of a man who has committed suicide by hanging.

Chapter 13

Sapphites, Flagellation and Cross-dressers

Sapphites

Whereas it is possible to talk about a 'gay scene' in the eighteenth century, especially in parts of London where molly-houses were not uncommon, it is too strong to refer to a lesbian scene, in the sense that lesbian relationships were far more secretive. Besides, most books and commentaries were written by men, and it is fair to say that most men just didn't 'get' lesbian behaviour. ('How would that work? Surely you need a man for that'). So, lesbianism was rarely featured in novels or in the press, and was never actually illegal. That is not to say that women who enjoyed a close friendship with each other were not subject to ridicule and gossip.

Take Hester Thrale's comments when she described the sculptress Anne Damer as a 'Lady much suspected for liking her own Sex in a

The Discovery, by Thomas Rowlandson.

criminal way', and alleging that she pursued the actress Elizabeth Farren. Damer also had a close relationship with the writer Mary Berry, and both regularly wore men's clothing. One observer of the closeness between Anne Damer and Mary Berry was Joseph Farrington who wrote in his 1798 diary that: 'The singularities of Mrs Damer are remarkable — She wears a Mans Hat, and Shoes, — and a Jacket also like a mans — thus she walks ab[ou]t. the fields with a hooking stick ... The extasi[e]s on meeting, and tender leave on separating, between Mrs Damer and Miss Berry, is whimsical. On Miss [Mary] Berry going lately to Cheltenham, the servants described the separation between Her and Mrs Damer as if it had been parting before death.'

There appear to have been a number of actresses who preferred the company of women to other men, with the traveller Archenholz commenting that: 'There are females who avoid all intimate intercourse with the opposite sex. These females are called Lesbians. They have small societies, known as Anandrinic Societies, of which Mrs Y..., formerly a famous London actress, was one of the presidents.'

For 'Mrs Y' read Mary Anne Yates, with another associate being the actress Kitty Clive. The common link with all these women was their close friendship with the aesthete Horace Walpole, otherwise known as the 4th Earl of Orford. Anne Damer was Walpole's main beneficiary under his will, whereas Mary Berry was his executor and for the last sixteen years of her life Kitty Clive lived in a cottage at Strawberry Hill donated to her by Walpole. But where were the other 'anandrinic societies'? There may have been other small groups of artists and actresses who shared similar sexual proclivities (referred to in literature as 'the game of flats') but there are no written records and, because lesbianism was not unlawful, there are of course no court records.

So, it may have been acceptable for two women to be seen arm-in-arm in public, or exchanging affectionate kisses, in a manner which two men would have found to be impossible without being denounced for outrageous immorality. That did not mean that there was a lack of homophobia. All instances of female closeness would have earned the disapproval of the Hester Thrale, who commented that 'Sapphists [...] deserve to be thrown [...] into Mount Vesuvius.' This was probably a widely-held view among the public. John Cleland's *Memoirs of a Lady of*

Pleasure was unusual in that it described the pleasure of sex; including sex between women.

During her first night in Mrs Brown's brothel, Fanny is initiated into the world of sexual pleasure by Phoebe, another girl who lives at the bawdy house. This would not so much have shocked readers as surprised them – surprised at the idea that a woman could derive pleasure from sex, without a man being involved. To the Georgians, sex first and foremost involved a penis. No penis – no great interest.

In the eighteenth century, unlike our own, two women could set up home together without the automatic assumption of sapphism. Take the Ladies of Llangollen, for example. The epithet was given to Lady Charlotte Eleanor Butler and Sarah Ponsonby, after they had fled from Ireland in order to avoid being forced into loveless marriages. There is no doubt that theirs was a romantic love affair that lasted a lifetime, but whether it ever strayed into a physical relationship is far from clear. Modern writers see their cohabiting as a splendid early example of two lesbians succeeding in a world on their own terms. They would probably have been horrified at the suggestion that they were anything other than two people who adored each other's company, and who were able to survive by pooling financial resources. They became a *cause célèbre* at the time, visited by all the leading writers, poets and do-gooders of the age. Byron, Shelley and Wordsworth all paid visits to observe at firsthand what was obviously seen as an extraordinary domestic arrangement. They were called upon by Anna Seward, a sapphic poetess who enjoyed the title of 'the Swan of Lichfield'. They were feted by Erasmus Darwin and Josiah Wedgwood, and by the Wordsworths.

They also had a strong influence on Anne Lister, who visited them from her home in Yorkshire. Anne went on to enter into a form of marriage with her female lover, no doubt inspired by the living arrangements and courage of the Llangollen Ladies. Anne kept a diary; one of the very few from the Georgian era that openly recorded lesbian affairs. Known to contemporaries as 'Gentleman Jack', Anne Lister's diaries ran to some four million words and cover many years. Written in code, these are now regarded as an important source of information about lesbianism in the eighteenth and early nineteenth centuries. Above all, the fact that they were encoded, and not published until the present century, shows how secretive people were about same-sex relationships. It is also safe to assume that if such relationships occurred in Halifax, where Anne Lister lived, they occurred elsewhere throughout the country, but have passed unrecorded into history.

The two ladies of Llangollen each received a pension of fifty pounds a year from George III after the king's wife, Charlotte, had exchanged gardening tips. Surely none of this would have happened if there had been a hint or suspicion of gross immorality, which is how it would have been viewed if sex were involved. More compellingly, the pair were often visited by Hester Thrale, a woman who seemed to be able to sniff out immorality from a hundred paces. Not from her the complaint that the behaviour of her hostesses was in any way 'French' or 'wicked'. Hester's verdict? They were 'delightful ladies', and firm friends.

What is to be made of the celebrity status enjoyed by the Ladies of Llangollen? If they were lesbians they certainly knew that it was in their best interests to keep it well hidden. But in any event their fame shows how men considered themselves essential to any relationship, and marvelled that a relationship could exist without a man being involved. As with so many other things, the world was phallus-orientated and although the ladies of Llangollen largely escaped direct criticism, they were nonetheless oddities, ridiculed for their insistence on wearing riding habits, and of covering everything with perfume.

Similarly, take the relationship between Queen Anne and her two female favourites, Sarah Churchill and Sarah's cousin, Abigail Masham (née Hill). Much has been made of the suggestion that the friendship was physical, but there is no conclusive evidence for this. A woman who had become pregnant on no fewer than seventeen occasions, and who still shared a bed with her husband until he died in October 1708, is surely entitled to have sought an escape from the stifling formality of Court by enjoying female friendship without being termed a lesbian.

We like to pigeon-hole people, especially for our own ends. So, much has been made of the 'two female pirates, Anne Bonny and Mary Read', the implication being that theirs was a lesbian relationship. It slightly overlooks the fact that when they were caught, on board the sloop *William* in 1720, they both successfully 'pleaded their bellies', i.e. by satisfying the court that they were pregnant. In Anne's case she had been the mistress of John Rackham, better known as Calico Jack. Modern stories show both women in men's clothing, but this is not substantiated by the few contemporaneous reports. The whole tale is embroidered to the extent that they are lauded as Amazonian figures; swashbuckling pirates who sailed the Seven Seas in search of fortune. The reality is that neither ever commanded a ship. They were members of the crew of a generally unsuccessful ship, serving under a small-time pirate captain with a dubious taste in wearing unbleached cotton. Calico Jack's entire pirate career had only lasted two years and his main success had been in capturing a handful of fishing vessels and ships with low-value cargoes. He was never particularly brave or ferocious, and reneged on his word when given a pardon by Governor Woodes Rogers. He was thirty-seven when he died.

As for Anne Bonny and Mary Read, their career in piracy lasted barely two months. More romantic twaddle has been written about them than the bare bones of their story can possibly justify. So, there seems little point in giving credence to the suggestion that the two women enjoyed a lesbian relationship, set up home together and grew roses in their south coast garden. A far more likely fate would have been that they both died in one of the prisons of Jamaica, which were not exactly renowned at that time as health spas.

What is probably true is that Mary Read had spent most of her life – and all of her childhood – as Mark Read, forced to impersonate her deceased brother by a mother who wanted to continue to receive an allowance from the boy's grandparents. As an adult she had found that dressing as a man opened doors not open to her as a woman, including joining the army. While serving in the army fighting the French alongside the Dutch, she had met a Flemish soldier and had fallen in love. The couple both left the army to run a public house at Breda known as the Three Horseshoes, but when her husband died and left her penniless Mary drifted into the merchant navy using a male persona. It was only when she was captured by Calico Jack that she revealed her gender, and the fact that she subsequently got pregnant surely points more to a relationship with one or more of the men on board the *William* rather than to any sort of affair with Anne Bonny. It has not stopped modern gay activists claiming Mary as one of their own.

At the time, there were prominent women in the public eye who evidently enjoyed a physical relationship with other women. One such was Lady Caroline, married to William Stanhope, the 2nd Earl Harrington. She may have had seven children by him, but that did not stop her founding the New Female Coterie, a group of *demimondaines* who met up regularly at Sarah Prendergast's high-class seraglio in Kings Place, St James's. Lady Caroline's insatiable sexual appetite and stamina led her to be called the 'Stable Yard Messalina' (after the debauched wife of the Emperor Claudius). She did not confine herself to the male visitors to the brothel, or indeed to her own footmen who were expected to perform duties not normally found in a servant's contract of employment, but also took female lovers, most notably Elizabeth Ashe. A leading bisexual of her day, she was mentioned in the *Town & Country Magazine* as someone who enjoyed affairs with 'lovers from a monarch down to a hairdresser and every member of the diplomatic body'.

Flagellation

One thing more than any other differentiates pornographic writings in the eighteenth century from the ballads, plays and books of the previous century: their reference to flagellation. Clearly, people suddenly felt able to laugh about what had previously been seen as 'unnatural behaviour', and to mock its adherents. In John Cleland's *Memoirs* Fanny describes in some detail the actions of Mr Barville who enjoyed thrashing her ('raising me on my knees, and making me kneel with them straddling wide, that tender part of me, naturally the province of pleasure, not pain, came in for its share of suffering: for now, eyeing it wistfully, he directed the rod so that the sharp ends of the twigs lighted there, so sensibly, that I could not help wincing, and writhing my limbs with pain.') But more often than not, the woman was the dominatrix employed by the man to thrash him. Shades of life at boarding school, to the extent that flagellation was regarded on the continent as being a peculiarly English activity and was termed 'the English vice'.

Beating men on the buttocks with a handful of birch twigs was apparently good for business, if the case of Theresa Berkley is anything to go by. She was a madam who ran a brothel in Marylebone and her

USP was a device called the Berkley Horse: a tilting board like a pair of step-ladders, with cut-out sections enabling the man (it was usually, but not exclusively, the man who was thrashed) to be tied securely in such a way that two women could 'work on him' at the same time, one administering the birch (or other 'instrument' according to taste) while the other woman, naked, sat below the man and pleasured him. Theresa called it a 'chevalet', and if a contemporary description is to be believed, she offered many of the experiences nowadays associated with BDSM (an abbreviation for Bondage and Discipline (BD), Dominance and Submission (DS), and Sadism and Masochism (SM)). The Victorian writer Henry Spencer Ashbee published a three-volume bibliography of erotic literature under the pseudonym of 'Pisanus Fraxi' and it contains the following description of Theresa Berkley:

> Her instruments of torture were more numerous than those of any other governess. Her supply of birch was extensive, and kept in water, so that it was always green and pliant: she had shafts with a dozen whip thongs on each of them; a dozen different sizes of cat-o'-nine-tails, some with needle points worked into them; various kinds of thin bending canes; leather straps like coach traces; battledoors, made of thick sole-leather, with inch nails run through to docket, and currycomb tough hides rendered callous by many years flagellation. Holly brushes, furze brushes; a prickly evergreen, called butcher's bush; and during the summer, a glass and China vases, filled with a constant supply of green nettles, with which she often restored the dead to life. Thus, at her shop, whoever went with plenty of money, could be birched, whipped, fustigated, scourged, needle-pricked, half-hung, holly-brushed, furze-brushed, butcher-brushed, stinging-nettled, curry-combed, phlebotomized, and tortured till he had a belly full.

What's not to like? If men had the money, and were so inclined, they could hire Theresa herself to be the person being flogged, although apparently she had a group of other women willing to take her place ('Miss Ring, Hannah Jones, Sally Taylor, One-eyed Peg, Bauld-cunted Poll, and a black girl called Ebony Bet'). On occasions women would pay to flog other women. Theresa made rather a lot of money pandering to such behaviour, and when she died she left an estate worth £100,000. Her brother, who had been a missionary spreading the word of the Lord amongst the 'heathen savages' of Australia for some thirty years, returned to Britain to claim his inheritance, blissfully unaware of how it had been earned. On learning the truth, he high-tailed it back to Australia without claiming the estate. It therefore passed in its entirety to the Crown via the Duchy of Lancaster.

Flagellation emporia were commonplace in eighteenth-century London, with the German writer Archenholz specifically mentioning the bagnios in Covent Garden ('Old people and degenerates can here receive flagellation for which all establishments are prepared'). The popularity of such treatments was reflected in literature throughout the century, from 1727 when Edward Curll was charged with obscene libel for publishing a translation of J.H. Meibomius's *Treatise on the use of flogging* through to *The Birchen Bouquet* (c.1770) and *Venus Schoolmistress* (1810). *The Exhibition of Female Flagellants* came out in two parts over a period of fourteen years between 1761 and 1785 and the full title goes on to say '*Proving from Indubitable Facts that a number of ladies take a secret pleasure in whipping their own.*'

Royalty and the aristocracy were particularly associated with a love of flogging, with the father of the future Queen Victoria (better known as Edward, Duke of Kent) having a reputation for getting his kicks out of watching a good flogging. At one stage he was put in charge of the garrison on Gibraltar, and was so keen on enforcing naval discipline, to the point of gratuitous torture, that the men mutinied and the duke was recalled to London in disgrace. When Theresa Berkley left her papers to her executor, Dr Vance, these apparently contained correspondence with a considerable number of people drawn from the upper echelons of society, including several males and females from the royal family. Sadly, Dr Vance chose to destroy what would have been a fascinating insight into the 'English Vice'.

Cross-dressing

It is clear that cross-dressing was not unknown in the eighteenth century, and perhaps not surprisingly, when society offered so many more advantages for men than women, the majority of cross-dressers were women choosing to live their lives as men, rather than the other way round. The literature and ballads of the day are full of stories of young girls running away to join the army so as not to be parted from their male lovers. Some may even have been true, such as the story of Phoebe Hessel. Her gravestone in a church in Brighton bears the inscription:

> In memory of Phoebe Hessel, who was born at Stepney in the year 1713. She served for many years, as a private soldier in the 5th Regiment of Foot, in different parts of Europe, and in the year 1745 fought under the command of the Duke of Cumberland at the Battle of Fontenoy, where she received a bayonet wound in the arm. Her long life, which commenced in the reign of Queen Anne, extended to George the Fourth, by whose munificence she received comfort and support in her latter years. She died at Brighton, where she had long resided, December 12, 1821, aged 108 years and lies buried here.

Doubts may well be justified about the entire veracity of the memorial, but it certainly looks as though Phoebe did join the army, dressed as a man, and was awarded an army pension when she returned to civilian duties. Her case echoes that of Margaret Ann Bulkley, better known as James Barry, who had attended medical school in Edinburgh dressed as a man, and who later rose through the ranks in the army to become Inspector General in charge of various military hospitals. Only after her death at the age of seventy-six was her real gender revealed.

Other cases of cross-dressing, carried out with the intention to deceive, include marriages between two women where one had adopted a male persona. It may be hard to credit, but in some cases the deception lasted for a considerable time, presumably because the 'male' partner availed herself of a strap-on device. Perhaps most extreme was the case of Mary Hamilton (who also went under the name of William, or George, or Charles Hamilton). She was tried at Taunton in 1746 for fraudulently posing as a man and marrying a woman. The writer Henry Fielding subsequently published a highly fictionalised account of the story as *The Female Husband: or, The Surprising History of Mrs Mary, alias Mr George Hamilton*.

The Fielding story is interesting not because it is an accurate record (it certainly was not) but because it reveals the misogynistic and prurient views of the author. He describes Hamilton as a 'wicked woman' with 'vile amours', one who resorted to practices 'which decency forbids me even to mention'. The Fielding version has Mary Hamilton 'marrying' at least fourteen women right across the West Country. What is probably true is that Mary dressed as a man and went through a form of marriage ceremony with a Mary Price, of Wells, in 1746. Mary Price discovered the deception some two months afterwards and complained to the examining Justice of the Peace, deposing that the accused had 'entered her body several times'. This 'made this examinant believe, at first, that the said Hamilton was a real man, but soon had reason to judge that the said Hamilton was not a man, but a woman'. The verdict of the court was that 'he or she prisoner at the bar is an uncommon, notorious cheat, and we, the Court, do sentence her, or him, whichever he or she may be, to be imprisoned six months, and during that time to be whipped in the towns of Taunton, Glastonbury, Wells, and Shepton Mallet.'

The case was by no means unique. *The Daily Advertiser* of 8 July 1777 reported on a similar prosecution in London: 'On Saturday last a Woman was convicted at the Guildhall, Westminster, for going in Men's Cloaths, and being married to three different Women by a fictitious Name, and for defrauding them of the Money and Cloaths: She was sentenced to stand in the Pillory at Charing-Cross, and to be imprisoned six Months.'

Clearly the cases say much about the ignorance and gullibility of young women in the Georgian era. In practice the use of dildos had featured in broadsheets, plays and ballads throughout the seventeenth and early eighteenth century, and their use is described in more detail in Chapter 5.

But deception apart, cross-dressing became a central part of entertainment, especially in London, with the development of the masquerade. Masquerade balls had first been introduced to London in the seventeenth century. The first of these promiscuous and fashionable assemblages was organized by a Swiss count by the name of John James Heidegger and was held at London's Haymarket. Anyone who could afford a ticket could attend a masquerade ball, and that was most unusual because it meant that masked commoners were allowed to hob-nob with the masquerading elite. We tend to equate masquerades with fancy dress parties, but the masquerades were much more sexually charged affairs than mere fancy dress. Here, men could adopt a female persona and explore their own sexuality, flirting and play-acting out their fantasies. Women of all classes could choose who they wanted to be: the duchess as a shepherdess, the milliner as a noble lord.

Masquerades were extremely popular. Some were held in private homes, by invitation only, but public masquerades were held at Vauxhall Gardens and at the Pantheon, which had opened in 1772. The main rotunda was one of the largest rooms built in England up to that time, and had a central dome somewhat reminiscent of the celebrated Pantheon in Rome: hence its name. The fashionable season at the Pantheon began in December or January and ended in April or May. Subscribers paid six guineas for admission to the twelve assemblies, which began at about seven o'clock. There were several masquerades in each season, and the building was elaborately decorated for these occasions. Sometimes these masked balls were sponsored by one of the fashionable clubs: Boodle's in 1774, Goostree's in 1775, and White's in 1789. Twelve subscription concerts also formed part of the seasonal round and at the conclusion of each concert there was dancing.

But one problem dogged the masquerade: its association with prostitution and lewd behaviour. To start with, the Pantheon organizers tried to make the place very exclusive. Guests were not allowed in unless invited by a peer of the realm. This was most unpopular with the leading courtesans of the day, who wished to go there to pick up custom but found themselves barred from entering.

Then one day in January 1776 Lord Cholmondeley turned up at the Pantheon with not just one but two of the leading hookers of the day: Dally the Tall (the nickname for Grace Dalrymple Elliott) and the diminutive Gertrude Mahon, better known as the Bird of Paradise, mentioned in Chapter 4. The trio walked up and demanded entry, and faced with His Lordship's backing, the stewards gave way. From then on there was no control, and masquerades rapidly became associated with lewd and immoral behaviour.

Ranelagh (a public pleasure gardens located in Chelsea) was another venue celebrated for its masquerade balls. The first one was given on 24 May 1759 to mark the birth of the Prince of Wales. Sometimes there was gambling and sometimes just entertainment with singers, dancers, or actors performing. Horace Walpole wrote soon after the gardens opened, 'It has totally beat Vauxhall [...] You can't set your foot without treading on a Prince, or the Duke of Cumberland.'

Until then, the masquerade ball had been mostly a private aristocratic entertainment, but Ranelagh brought it to a wider, middle-class English public. The balls usually started late in the evening and meals were served anywhere from midnight to two, three, or even four in the morning. Most revellers headed for home by half past six. Wearing elaborate disguises, London's rich, famous and infamous would meet to dance, flirt and intrigue until the early hours of the morning.

Despite their popularity and glamour, masquerades were seen by some as immoral, scandalous and unpatriotic. They were publicly denounced by the Bishop of London, and on 6 January 1724 a sermon was preached by him which 'produced so great an effect [...] orders were issued, that there should be no more such amusements than had been already subscribed for at the beginning of the month, which were six.'

This marked the emergence of the anti-masquerade protestors — clergymen, moralists, and journalists — who argued that masquerade balls were salacious events that encouraged immorality and sexual transgression, as well as homosexuality, adultery, and prostitution. What really sent critics into a panic was the idea of disguise, and the implications of being disguised. Within the walls of the masquerade, the formal conventions of polite eighteenth-century society were suspended. With the right costume, and a mask to hide your true identity, it was possible to step into another world for a few hours, where men dressed as women and vice versa, prostitutes disguised themselves as nuns, and Englishmen became Ottoman Turks in robes and turbans. No wonder cross-dressing scandalised polite society. It was seen as undermining the very fabric upon which society was built.

A look at cross-dressing has to include mention of a man who has subsequently been described as the first true intersex person in Britain: the so-called Chevalier d'Eon. French born, a spy, a freemason, a soldier, a diplomat and an extrovert, d'Eon had come to London as *chargé d'affaires* in April 1763. His androgynous features led to speculation that 'he' was actually 'she' and d'Eon played up to this by dressing as a woman, claiming that he had been born a girl but had been forced to pose as a boy just so that his father could inherit from his parents-in-law. From 1777 he spent thirty-three years in female clothing, and after his death a post mortem examination suggested that he was probably intersex: in other words, he exhibited certain female characteristics in addition to having male genitalia.

In his lifetime he fascinated polite society, was the subject of wagers as to his gender, and was even promoted as a shining example of female fortitude, to which all women could aspire, by proto-feminists such as Mary Robinson and Mary Wollstonecraft. D'Eon enjoyed a remarkable celebrity status; the first person to be openly transvestite in British history.

Chevalier d'Eon. (see also Plate 2)

Chapter 14

Sex and Sexuality in Eighteenth-century Literature and Art

There have been many nominations put forward for the title of 'the first English novel' but one thing is clear: the eighteenth century saw the emergence of the novel as a most effective literary means to describe emotions and desires, to comment on prevailing social conditions and to highlight attitudes towards sex and sexuality. Whether the first novelist was Aphra Behn or John Bunyan, whether it was Daniel Defoe or Samuel Richardson, or someone else totally forgotten, is not

A duet on the piano ....

important here: what matters is that consciously or unconsciously the authors of novels give a fascinating insight into the prevailing morality of the period.

Starting not with a novel but with a book published in 1749 – the very same year that Cleland introduced Fanny Hill to the startled world – Peter Annet's *Social Bliss Considered* gives an antidote to the earlier ideas put forward by the established church that sex was inherently wicked. Annet was an interesting if little-known figure. Originally a schoolmaster, he used his analytical mind to trawl through the Bible, asking the question, 'Where does it say that?' Where did it say that divorce was wrong? Where did it say that fornication was sinful? Where did it say that being paid for sex was wrong? In the latter case he argued that whoring was not the evil; that the evil was the poverty which drove women into prostitution.

He was particularly articulate in his criticism of marriages 'sanctified' by sham pastors operating within the confines of the Fleet prison, writing in *Social Bliss Considered*: 'If the end of marriage be answered, viz the benefit of society and posterity, where's the piety in contending for a superstitious ceremony? And where's the virtue of it, when a sham or scoundrel parson at the Fleet shall so bind the holy noose that the greatest unholiness cannot dissolve it?' Annet argued that divorce was preferable to forcing a couple to remain married against their wishes and in doing so, echoed the words of John Milton a hundred years earlier.

Annet recognized the importance of virginity, and argued that a man who 'defloured a virgin under pretence of marriage was a fraud and a knave.' In his view, to 'tempt a virgin or a virtuous matron to transgress laws of chastity and constancy is not less a crime than defrauding one of his property.' That may seem obvious, but in a world which laid all the blame on the woman for being promiscuous and unable to resist her carnal desires, it is refreshing to hear someone lay the blame firmly at the door of the male. Elsewhere in the same book he gave the opinion: 'Where neither party injure each other, but a man's natural appetite is satisfy'd by the use of an obliging Courtezan, if he is under no legal ties to another that ought in reason to restrain him, but pleasure is mutually given and received, I cannot see any evil to be in the action more than in the desire […] the desire of mutual enjoyment is natural to maturity, health and an uncorrupted and vigorous constitution.' Here was his answer to those who argued, 'He that cannot refrain, let him marry.'

Poor Annet: he may have argued in favour of sexual freedom, and sought to counter the medieval idea that sex was basically sinful and should only be permitted within a marriage between a man and a woman, but he fell foul of the authorities when his questioning mind went one stage further and he challenged the truth of the stories in the Old Testament. For that, he was hauled before Lord Mansfield in 1762 and charged with blasphemous libel. Annet was by then seventy years old and the court recognized his frailty, and poverty, and took a 'more lenient, humane view' of his offences. The court in their charitable wisdom therefore sent Annet to prison for a year's hard labour, sentenced him to two spells in the pillory, fined him, and obliged him to find sureties for his good behaviour. Annet ultimately returned to being a teacher, and died in 1769, but not before he had bravely republished – in 1766 – all of his earlier writings as an omnibus edition under the title of *A Collection of Tracts of a Certain Free Enquirer noted by his sufferings for his opinions.*

There were, of course, other commentators and pamphlet writers who called for greater sexual freedom, and who wanted to address the underlying problems of poverty and social deprivation which lay behind prostitution – just as there were clergymen willing to argue that all sex outside of marriage was sinful, and that writing about sex was corrupting public morals – and causing earthquakes.

When the book, *A dialogue between a Married Lady and a Maid*, was published in 1740 it continued the tradition dating from the previous century of showing two women talking about sex in such a way that it was calculated to arouse male interest, while masquerading as a female advice column. Meanwhile, the collected works of the Earl of Rochester, bawdy, crude and occasionally mildly erotic, were republished at various stages (in 1718, 1739 and 1752). Ned Ward's *The Pleasures of a Single Life* had appeared in 1709, while the 1721 publication of *The Life of the late celebrated Mrs Elizabeth Wisebourn* proved to be a fascinating account of events at an elegant London brothel, presided over by Madam Wybourn. Its success spawned a raft of similar prostitute tell-all books published throughout the Georgian era and culminating in the publication of *The Memoirs of Harriette Wilson, Written By Herself* in 1825. It lifted the lid on the illustrious career of Harriette Wilson, the leading courtesan of the Regency period and offered its voyeuristic readers an insight into the sexual exploits of their social superiors, from the Duke of Wellington to the Marquess of Worcester, from Lord Craven to Lord Ponsonby. Thirty editions of the memoirs came out in the first year alone, and became a multi-volume book when translated into French. The memoirs made a small fortune for Harriette, quite apart from the money she made from blackmailing her clients in return for guaranteeing their anonymity. Pornography and stories about sex and sexual goings-on proved to be a bestselling tradition throughout the reigns of the first four Georges.

In 1739 a sensational book had been published consisting of the report of the trial of William Soper in an action for what was known as 'criminal conversation', brought by Theophilus Cibber. It was, in effect, the precursor of a divorce trial and gave intimate details of the alleged adultery committed by Mrs Cibber. Reading the book it is easy to get the impression that maids and manservants alike spent a considerable amount of their time drilling holes in doors and wainscot panelling in order to observe the adulterous goings-on of their employers. It was a sort of double voyeurism: the servants clearly enjoyed watching other people fornicate, and the general public then bought the trial reports so that they too could derive a vicarious pleasure from reading about it. To modern tastes these prurient reports, set down as trial reports, may seem somewhat tame and artificial, but many eighteenth-century readers found them titillating and worthy of the expense (sixpence). The popularity of the book led to other trial reports, all avidly followed by the public and ending up in a seven-volume *oeuvre* brought out under the title of *Trials for adultery*, or, *The history of Divorces* in seven volumes ('taken in shorthand, by a Civilian') published in 1779–80.

The word 'pornography' did not enter mainstream English language until the 1850s and derives from two Greek words meaning, literally, a written description or illustration of prostitutes or prostitution. In its currently accepted sense of meaning erotic writings, these had, of course, been around for centuries. The seventeenth century saw an explosion of bawdy writings and erotic works intended to titillate and arouse male readers (usually masquerading as advice to young ladies, such as the 1684 *Aristotle's Masterpiece*). But the middle of the eighteenth century saw the publication of the extraordinary *Memoirs of a Lady of Pleasure*, nowadays better known as *Fanny Hill*. It is one of the most banned books in English literature and is generally recognized as the first English pornographic novel. Within a year of publication both the author, John Cleland, and the publisher, Ralph Griffiths, were hauled before the Court, charged with 'corrupting the King's subjects', and although Cleland renounced the book and asked for it to be officially withdrawn, pirated copies were soon being printed.

For over two centuries the book 'went underground', resurfacing as recently as 1963 when Gareth Powell of the publishing firm of Mayflower Books was charged under Section 3 of the 1959 Obscene Publications Act. No matter that his defence was that the work was a historical sourcebook and simply reflected the joy of sex, Powell was convicted because the book described what was seen as a sexual perversion: in this case, flagellation. It was not until 1970 that a further uncensored version of the book appeared in print in Britain. The Obscene Publications Act, modified in 1964, is still on the statute book but clearly modern views on obscenity have changed. After holding a public consultation, the Crown Prosecution Service issued guidelines in 2019 to the effect that pornography depicting consenting adults engaged in legal acts would no longer be prosecuted under the act, just so long as no serious harm was caused and provided that the likely audience was over the age of eighteen. The guidelines also made it clear that even if material is deliberately and clearly obscene it can be justified as being in the public good if it is 'in the interests of science, literature, art or learning.'

So why, historically, was *Fanny Hill* such a banned and yet groundbreaking novel? More than anything else, because the heroine escapes unscathed from her life of sexual freedom. Modern writers may condemn its image of the 'happy hooker' and certainly it is very much a man's view of a woman having a great romp through life, under the bedclothes. There is no degradation, no rape, no torture, no venereal disease: just lots of sex and lots of different sorts of sex. All are enjoyed by our heroine, but she finally concludes that sexual pleasure is at its greatest when it is within a loving relationship. In that sense it epitomises the feeling that developed in the eighteenth century: that personal freedoms should not be subject to State or Ecclesiastical control, and that men, and importantly women, had every right to seek out pleasure wherever and whenever they wanted, with whomever they chose.

Cleland was not of course the first to say that a woman had the right to control her own body. In that sense Daniel Defoe's *Roxana*, published in 1724, was an important milestone, one that invited the reader not to judge the heroine for being a prostitute, but to accept that her circumstances gave her no alternative. She did not ask her husband to run off, leaving her with children to bring up, and no income. She provides sexual services to her landlord in lieu of rent, to enable her to keep a roof over her head. Her life then leads her, through various twists and turns, to become a high-class courtesan in Pall Mall. In time she regrets her life as a mistress and a whore, remarries and goes to live in Holland but is pursued by the elder daughter of her first marriage, who wishes to confront her mother and thereby expose her.

The book contains the famous line, 'the Marriage Contract is [...] nothing but giving up Liberty, Estate, Authority, and everything, to the Man.' The story of Roxana reveals the inherent difficulty of a woman pursuing sexual freedom while avoiding pregnancy, and in the end we see Roxana facing ruin because of the actions of one of her children. The ending is deliberately ambiguous, but in facing up to the triple conflict between financial necessity on the first part, honour and reputation on the second part, and personal honesty on the other part, the book shows that sexual freedom came at a price.

Defoe had published *Moll Flanders* two years earlier than *Roxana*. That, too, was interesting in showing a woman as a heroine – a woman who married five times, was a kept mistress, and had a dozen children – all while living life as a thief and a confidence trickster. It is a romp, with an undercurrent of incest running through it from start to finish and, most unusually for literature of the period: it all ends happily-ever-after. Eighteenth-century readers may have been shocked to see that Moll never got her comeuppance for such an immoral life but at least Defoe was trying to look at life through the eyes of the female character. She was a survivor and she did what she had to in order to survive in a man's world.

All the authors mentioned so far have been male: what of the female writers and how do they show female sexuality? Interestingly, the two obvious female writers (Fanny Burney and Jane Austen) were hardly in a position to talk about the joys of passionate sex. In Fanny's case she wrote

Evelina in 1778 and *Cecilia* in 1782, a decade before she married, and there is no reason to believe that she had led anything other than a chaste life as a singleton. Her books were mostly about the importance of virtue in a woman and the need to steer a moral path through life. They are about male hypocrisy, about female oppression, about social expectations and the importance of making a good marriage. Fanny did write two novels after she got married (*Camilla* in 1796 and *The Wanderers* in 1814) but both followed the same path as the earlier books. The heroines of Fanny's novels definitely do not sleep around, experiment with dildos, share sapphic encounters or line up suitors and judge them by their physical attributes.

In much the same way, Jane Austen (a keen supporter of Fanny's works) wrote about women not as sexual creatures but as individuals who were entirely dependent upon making a good marriage. Jane never married and it is hard to believe that she was sexually experienced, and certainly not with a man. At one stage she had fallen in love with Tom Lefroy. He was twenty, and Jane was a year younger. Lefroy later went on to become Lord Chief Justice of Ireland, and confessed many years later that he had been in love with Jane, but that it was 'boyish love'. There is no suggestion that their love was ever consummated. On another occasion she was briefly engaged to a family friend, but she broke it off after just one day. Small wonder that Jane's works concentrate on love and mutual companionship and support, rather than on sexual fulfilment and lust.

Both Austen and Burney satirized male standards, especially among the landed gentry of turn-of-the-century Britain. Neither author wrote explicitly about sex and although both women wrote superb social commentaries, the total absence of sex makes them seem more Victorian than Georgian.

Less prudish, and far more revealing about prevailing promiscuity and licentiousness, were the caricaturists. The first half of the Georgian era was dominated by William Hogarth, whose satires are immaculately drawn. You can almost hear Hogarth shouting 'Don't do it. And if you do this is what will happen to you!' In his works we see the finger-wagging moralist pointing out the dangers of female promiscuity with his *A Harlot's Progress* in 1732. The male viewpoint was *A Rake's Progress* (first printed in 1735) and the folly of the upper classes in marrying for money was parodied in *Marriage a la Mode* (1743–45). Together they show the full panoply of immoral behaviour, from sexual excesses to drinking and gambling, and with all the characters succumbing to disease, poverty and degradation.

The contrast between Hogarth and later satirists is fascinating. Robert Newton mixed with whores in the area near Drury Lane, where he was born in 1777. He only lived to the age of twenty-one, but as a young man drew the people who he saw around him: especially fun-loving, often voluptuous, women. Sex, gambling and drinking were not to be censured, they were there to be enjoyed. Had he lived, Newton would have been a fabulous commentator on life at the turn of the century, but sadly he caught typhus and died in 1798.

James Gillray had been born twenty years before Newton. Described as 'the father of the political cartoon', he specialized in poking fun at the royal family, at leading politicians and other prominent figures. Oddly, he rarely took aim at sexual peccadilloes, more often opting for lavatorial humour and bawdy jokes rather than showing sexual activity. Occasionally, he showed his targets in sexual situations in order to parody them: as with *Sin Death and the Devil*, shown on page x, and *Fashionable Contrasts* on page vi. The latter was a direct response to the sycophantic behaviour of the press towards the wedding of the Duke and Duchess of York in September 1791. Endless column inches had been devoted to the daintiness of the feet of Frederica Charlotte Ulrica, Duchess of York. In response, Gillray published his satire in January 1792. It shows the entwined feet of the couple, clearly in a copulatory position, and it stopped the endless discussions stone-dead.

But if these were the exceptions that proved the Gillray rule, no one can say that Thomas Rowlandson held back from parodying sex in all its glory. Born in 1756 he honed his artistic skills drawing naked whores, fornicating housemaids, copulating footmen, and dirty old men leering at posture molls. The contrast between Hogarth and Rowlandson is plain. Hogarth, in *A Rake's Progress*, had shown a posture moll, fully dressed, preparing to take up position over a large pewter platter, which was intended to mirror her subsequent nakedness. It is not in any way obscene or erotic. Rowlandson has no such inhibitions and goes into close-up. He gives us the girl, completely naked and lying on her back with her bare buttocks in the air, while three elderly men examine her genitalia. The title, *Cunnyseurs*, is a pun on 'connoisseurs' and 'cunny', the eighteenth-century slang for a woman's vulva. As an aside, the posture molls set themselves as a class apart from prostitutes: they adopted poses, and performed in public houses for the titillation of male audiences, but did not necessarily have sex with the punters. Emma Hamilton, later to become the mistress of Horatio Nelson, almost certainly started out as a posture moll working for Charlotte Hayes in her fashionable King's Place brothel.

Rowlandson may have intended his erotica to be bought by men eager to build up a portfolio of indecent images, to be examined and 'appreciated' at a later date. But what they show is that in Rowlandson's world sex was everywhere, and it was there to be enjoyed by young and old alike. He particularly drew servants having a rare old time 'below stairs', but the one thing about Rowlandson's images is that they are general, not personal. Gillray lampooned individuals and made sure that the public knew who he was ridiculing, whereas Rowlandson was less specific and instead preferred to hold up his mirror to society as a whole.

There were a host of other caricaturists showing the sexual side of life, especially in London, for this was considered the Golden Age of Satire. It was an age that changed abruptly when Queen Victoria ascended the throne. Jokes about the sexual proclivities of debauched monarchs such as George IV and William IV may have been funny, but the same joke at the expense of an eighteen-year-old queen would not have been acceptable. The pendulum between good taste and bawdiness was to swing firmly in favour of decorum.

Setting aside the caricaturists, conventional painters have left us with innumerable portraits of 'women who should have known better'. Reynolds painted the actress-whore Frances Abington on at least six occasions, while George Romney was obsessed with painting Emma Hamilton and she became his constant muse. High-class courtesans such as Mary Robinson were the arbiters of fashion, and she had her portrait painted so many times that it is a wonder she had any time left for entertaining. Artists reflected the world around them: these were the top purveyors of sex, and sex was everywhere. And so the portraits of the sex workers ended up being displayed at exhibitions, such as the Summer

Exhibition of the Royal Academy, alongside the portraits of the great and the good, the duchesses and the princesses. Beauty and physical attractiveness were there for all to see, giving the chance for the working-class girls to strut their stuff alongside their social superiors.

To end with, no discussion about the eighteenth-century preoccupation with sex, whether in art or literature, is complete without mentioning John Wilkes and his notoriously filthy poem *An Essay on Woman*. The events surrounding the publication involves a cast list that would stretch the credulity of the public even in the hands of an accomplished writer. It included John Potter, the Archbishop of Canterbury and his son, Thomas, who was an MP and a rake of the first order. He was also a man who spent much of his energy in bed with the wife of a certain Dr William Warburton. Well, not all his energies, as apparently he was once spotted fornicating with a cow on Wingrove Common.

Dr Warburton owned the rights to publish Alexander Pope's *An Essay on Man* and had contributed lengthy and ponderous marginal notes to Pope's work after it first came out in 1733. Then there was John Wilkes, something of an innocent-at-large at that stage, but someone who was led astray by Thomas Potter. Both were members of the notorious Hellfire Club, which met at Medmenham Abbey, where members were renowned for their sexual excesses. Ironically, one of the other members of the club was John Montagu, Fourth Earl of Sandwich. The earl had at one stage been on friendly terms with Wilkes, although this friendship evaporated after a number of practical jokes carried out by Wilkes at his expense.

Potter had amused himself by starting to write an obscene parody about Pope's *Essay*, under the title of *An Essay on Woman*, dedicating it to the famous courtesan Fanny Murray (known to have been a mistress of the Earl of Sandwich). The parody extended to the pompous notes written by Dr Warburton. When Potter died in 1759 his papers were inherited by Wilkes, who probably added to the obscene lyrics and appears to have had a dozen copies printed up for distribution among his Hellfire Club friends.

Following a police raid on his premises the authorities seized the manuscript and decided to use this to discredit Wilkes, who by then was gaining fame for his anti-monarchy and anti-government views. To strengthen the allegation of obscene libel the authorities inserted

Sex and Sexuality in Eighteenth-century Literature and Art   163

additional and blasphemous passages into the already lewd text and had additional copies printed in order to suggest that the entire work had been published by Wilkes (and not merely circulated on a private basis). At that stage the Earl of Sandwich, who was by then Secretary of State, tried to blackmail Wilkes into giving up his civil rights litigation against the government in return for dropping libel and blasphemy charges against Wilkes, but Wilkes refused and he soon found himself facing charges of sedition before the House of Commons and libel in the House of Lords.

The alleged libel was against none other than Dr Warburton, who by then was sitting in the Lords in his capacity as Bishop of Gloucester. The case meant that the Earl of Sandwich, renowned as a whoring libertine, was required to read out the entire poem to their assembled

Cunnyseurs, by Thomas Rowlandson.

lordships, all of whom would have been well aware that Warburton had been cuckolded for many years by the late Thomas Potter. There was nothing subtle about it: the poem's cover apparently showed the image of an erect penis alongside a ten-inch ruler. Those eagerly listening to the lewd verses would have known who was the object of the poem's ridicule, particularly when it referred to prominent members of the government including Lord Bute and the Earl of Sandwich himself.

The poetry recital was met by howls of laughter and derision by their lordships, and led one commentator to remark that he 'never before heard the devil preach a sermon against sin'. The whole episode caused public outrage, not so much against Wilkes but against the government. As Horace Walpole remarked: 'The plot so hopefully laid to blow up Wilkes was so gross and scandalous, so revengeful and so totally unconnected with the political conduct of Wilkes, and the instruments so despicable, odious, or in whom any pretentions to decency, sanctimony or faith were so preposterous that, losing all sight of the scandal contained in the poem, the whole world almost united in crying out against the informers.'

The furore forced Wilkes to flee to France for five years, leaving Parliament to find him guilty *in absentia* and to declare him an outlaw. However, he returned to Britain in triumph in 1768, only to upset the applecart once more by standing for election as MP for Marylebone. Setting aside the political shenanigans, what this shows is that in the eighteenth century if people were not having sex, they were writing about sex, reading about sex, or using sex as a means to discredit or blackmail their enemies. Then, as now, sex sells.

Conclusion

The Georgian era was certainly a time of excess – excessive gambling, excessive drinking, excessive gluttony – and arguably, excessive sexual activity. But unlike subsequent periods when hypocrisy dominated, the Georgians were remarkably open about their excesses, especially sexual ones. And those excesses led to a terrifying increase in incidents of venereal disease, affecting rich and poor, men and women, old and young alike.

Sex around a country cottage – in Rowlandson's world, sex was in full view both indoors and, especially, outdoors.

It was also a remarkably unjust world: women, especially married women, had few legal rights and were treated as chattels. If she tried to leave her husband, a wife had no rights of access to any children of the marriage: and if she left, then she was in a sort of social limbo until her husband died. The whole idea of a *demimonde* was built upon hypocrisy – its members were feted and admired, but its adherents were 'the great impure' – never to be admitted into polite society.

Many women were compelled to sell their bodies for economic reasons, and many young girls were tricked into a form of sex slavery, unable to escape from the rapacious demands of money-lending brothel-keepers. Children were not protected from paedophilia, and girls as young as eight could find themselves raped and abandoned to a fate where their only prospect was to become a child prostitute. Sex crimes were not generally regarded as being on a par with, say, the theft of property.

James Boswell felt able to write perfectly openly that on one occasion he forced himself upon a young woman who he met in the Strand ('I was much stronger than her; and *volens nolens* [i.e. whether she wanted to or not] pushed her up against the Wall.'). As far as Boswell was concerned, she had accepted sixpence from him, and he was therefore entitled to have sex with her. Besides, she was merely a 'profligate wretch' and this alone meant that she had forfeited the right to say 'no'.

It was a time of astonishing ignorance and injustice. Men had so little idea about pregnancy and its causes that they assumed that a woman physically was unable to conceive unless she had consented to sex. It therefore followed that if a woman became pregnant, after claiming to have been raped, then she could not have been raped. No wonder few rapes were reported, and even fewer resulted in conviction.

If an unmarried woman gave birth to a child it meant that all she could look forward to was a life in the shadows, probably destitute, unemployable, and unmarriageable. No wonder that a girl who found herself pregnant was likely to resort to taking poison, in doses large enough in many cases to kill both the foetus and the mother herself.

It was an era of huge extremes, nowhere greater than between the rich and the poor. For the rich, money meant that you could afford to buy anything, and if that meant breaking the law, then the chances are that your status and wealth would ensure your acquittal. And if it didn't?

Well, you could always flee to the continent and live out your days in the French sunshine: William Courtenay and Elizabeth Chudleigh are cases in point. But there were also extremes between town and country, between men and women, between healthy and sick. For every courtesan enjoying the high life, dressed in the latest fashions, driving in her phaeton drawn by matching horses and with liveried footmen running alongside, there were hundreds, if not thousands, of women living miserable lives in abject poverty, riddled with sexually transmitted diseases and shunned by society.

As now, it helped to be beautiful, particularly for women. Beauty opened all sorts of doors that were otherwise closed. And once a woman became famous for her beauty, once she had 'sacrificed her virtue' and become the 'Toast of the Town', she was immediately handed round a tiny circle of royalty and aristocrats.

Most of all, sex and sexuality in the eighteenth century was about men, and male lust. In previous centuries, the teachings of the church pointed to the sin of adultery, the wickedness of fornication, the evil of sexual promiscuity. By 1727 Daniel Defoe was writing that monogamy was 'a mere church imposition, a piece of witchcraft, and unreasonable'. He echoed the earlier views of a man who went on to become Lord Chancellor of Ireland, a man called John Bowes. He opined that 'the natural purpose of women was to be subservient to a man's lust'. Later writers such as David Hume went further, arguing that chastity served no useful purpose and that 'confinement of the appetite is not natural'. In his *Treatise on Human Nature* (expanded and modified in *An Enquiry concerning the Principles of Morals*) Hume put forward the view that lust was not sinful because it had 'such a strong connection with all the agreeable emotions'. To paraphrase: if it feels good, it must be good.

It was therefore the start of a period of sexual freedom, especially on the part of men. 'Loose women' were still despised, particularly by other women. But men, well, they were rakes and libertines, doing what came naturally, and promiscuity and adultery were not regarded as being as far down the scale of bad behaviour as, say, being drunk. The century saw occasional bursts of activity against sodomites and the odd moral crusade against prostitution, but by and large the Georgian era marked a drift towards personal choice and sexual freedom: at least for men. Don't forget, the House of Hanover started with a king who left his wife behind in Hanover, locked up in a castle for thirty years because she had had the audacity to take a male lover. Instead, George I paraded his two mistresses at court when he arrived in London in 1714. And the Georgian era ended with William IV, a man who happily lived with his mistress, Dorothea Jordan, and who fathered ten children by her, only to drop her like a ton of bricks after two decades together when it suited him to get a wife and assume the role of monarch. There was a law for the rich, and there was a law for the poor. There was one law for men, and there was another law for women.

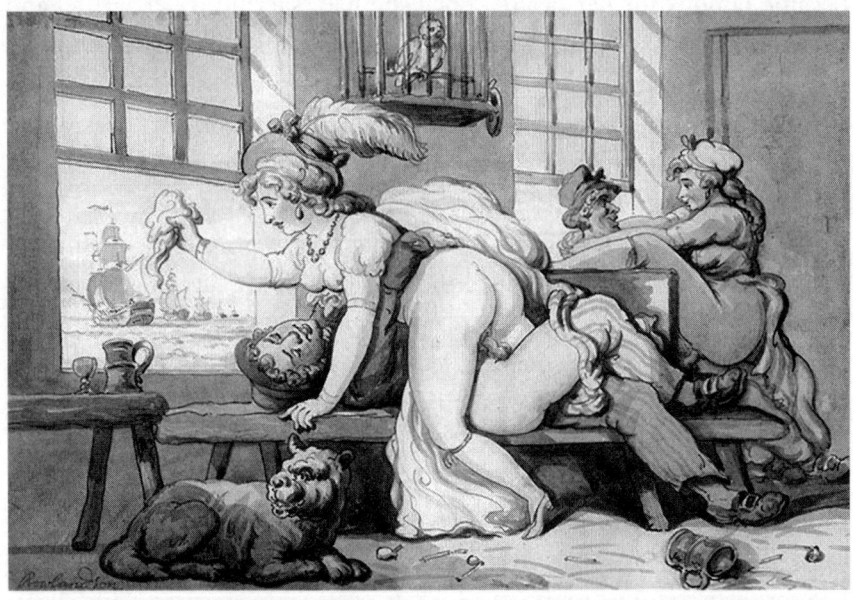

'Goodbye'

Appendix I

1. The trial of Captain Jones

In 1772 a sensational case involving the accusation of sodomy against a boy of thirteen came before the Old Bailey. It was to become the eighteenth-century equivalent to the trial of Oscar Wilde a hundred years later and it triggered a huge public debate about sodomy, about effeminacy, about foreignness and about being English. First, the trial report as it appeared in the *General Evening Post* of 21–23 July 1772:

Captain Jones, otherwise known as the Firework Macaroni.

An Account of the TRIAL *of* Capt. ROBERT JONES, *on Saturday last, at the Sessions-House in the Old-Bailey, for committing an unnatural and detestable crime on the person of* Henry-Francis Hay, *a boy about thirteen years of age.*

THE first evidence called was the boy on whom the crime was committed, who deposed that about a month ago he met with the prisoner at the bar (whom he had previously a slight knowledge of, from formerly living in that neighbourhood) in St. Martin's-lane; that he persuaded him to go with him to his lodgings, under a pretence of matching a knee buckle (the boy being apprentice to his uncle, who was a jeweller); that he accordingly went; that upon entering the room, the prisoner locked the door, and then *committed* the crime charged in the indictment on him; – that, after this, the prisoner gave him some halfpence, said that he could not find the buckle then, but desired he would call again next day, and tell no-body of what was done to him; that the boy accordingly went the next day, when he (the prisoner) repeated the same unnatural intercourse in every respect but the *last.* The boy being interrogated by the Court why he went the second day, as it was against his consent he was thus treated, he replied, he was partly tempted by the money the Captain promised him, as well as deterred from speaking of it to his uncle from shame, and the fear of his losing a good customer. In the course of the examination of this evidence, the Court received every *minute* satisfaction which the law required relative to the confirmation of that horrid fact.

The boy's uncle (a jeweller in St. Martin's Lane) was next examined, who deposed, that Capt. Jones, a few days after the commission of this crime (as he afterwards found out) came into his shop, and bought a shirt-buckle with some other things, and that he took notice the boy was rather shy of him; upon which he asked him why he did not speak to his old friend Captain Jones? That the boy made some evasive answer; and upon his asking him to carry the things home to the Captain's lodgings, he said he would rather be excused; that soon after he (the uncle) left the shop, when a Mr. Rapley being present, questioned the boy about his evasive answers to his uncle, when he confessed the whole affair in the same uniform manner he did in his evidence. He was asked by the Court what degree of reputation the boy's veracity stood in, or whether his character was good, or not? To which he answered, he never remembered to have found him in a lie in his life.

Mr. Rapley and Mr. Prest (two friends of the boy's uncle) were then severally examined, who both declared, that, on their separately questioning the boy, previous to their taking him before a Justice, in a very awful manner, setting before him not only the heinousness of telling a lye, but that of taking an innocent man's life away, which his evidence must do, if he swore falsely; he repeated the same story in every particular, except in a few trifling circumstances. These evidences were likewise called to the boy's character for veracity, who gave him a very good one.

This being the purport of the evidence against the prisoner, he was called upon his defence, who said no more than in general denying the charge, and calling some witnesses to his character, who gave him a very good one; and amongst these some women, who gave him the reputation of being a very *gallant* man amongst their sex. The Judge then summed up the whole of the evidence to the Jury; and, as he went along, very satisfactorily explained how far the fact was proved, as to the point of law; and that it entirely rested with them to decide, as they credited, or discredited the evidence. The Jury retired for about five minutes, and brought in their verdict: *guilty*. About five o'clock the same evening the prisoner was remanded to the dock, when the Recorder passed sentence of death on him, which he heard seemingly with great fortitude and composure; after it was finished he bowed, and retired.

During the course of this trial, where descriptions and phrases were necessarily made use of towards the legal ascertainment of the fact, that would, in any other place but a Court of Justice, make nature revolt, there was a number of well-dress'd women in the galleries, who sat very composedly the whole time, to the scandal of all decency and feminality.

Captain Jones was found guilty simply on the statements made by the boy, who waited three weeks after the alleged incident before revealing his story. There was no corroboration and no medical evidence was produced. The case gave rise to one of the first discussions about the whole offence of sodomy. Up until then it was sufficient to dismiss the crime as being unnatural and lewd, but here the court were asked to consider whether it was right that a man could be found guilty simply on the basis of an accusation, especially from a minor. After all, if the boy had been one year older (fourteen being the age of consent) Henry Francis Hay would himself have been liable to the charge of sodomy.

The lawyer for Jones argued, 'I say that no crime is to be punished but upon full Proof: and if you reply That it never will be proved; I say again, That it ought never to be punished.'

The case led to the publication of a pamphlet entitled *The State of the Case of Captain Jones*. It also provoked a storm of interest in the press. As one correspondent put it in a letter to the Public Ledger on August 5, 1772, Captain Jones, who was referred to as 'this Military Maccaroni' was 'too much engaged in every scene of idle Dissipation and wanton Extravagance'. The letter concluded with the words: 'therefore, ye Beaux, ye sweet-scented, simpering He-She things, deign to learn wisdom from the death of a Brother.'

Jones languished in Newgate prison amidst rumours of a Royal Pardon. He had been sentenced to death with a number of other men, all charged with different offences and on several occasions he would have listened to the sermon for the condemned man. On 4 August 1772 the *Manchester Mercury* informed its readers that: 'It is thought that Capt. Jones, who is now under Sentence of Death for an unnatural Crime, will received his Majesty's most gracious Pardon; as some Gentlemen of the first Rank and fortune in the County of Suffolk, as well as the celebrated Mr. Dryb—r and the whole Maccaroni Club, intend to convince a Great Personage that a Man of Taste should not lose his Life, for the Amore pio Pueri.'

Amore pio Pueri, meaning 'loyal love', was a phrase used by Virgil in *The Aeneid*: Samuel Drybutter was a notorious friend of Captain Jones, and he had been accused on several occasions of sodomitical practices and was generally reviled for his behaviour and appearance.

Not everyone was pleased to hear that a royal pardon was imminent. Disquiet spread from London throughout the countryside, with the *Salisbury and Winchester Journal* reporting that: 'The citizens of London may well tremble for fear, lest divine vengeance should make this city like Sodom and Gomorrah. – This nation had less to dread from Heaven if a thousand men, undiscovered, had been guilty of daily perpetrating this shameful crime, than for one man clearly and fully convicted, and solemnly condemned by the laws of this nation, to be pardoned.'

In the event the captain was granted a royal pardon on condition that he left the country, prompting a howl of protest led by people such as the radical Whig John Wilkes. He saw it as yet another example of corruption in government. If a poor man stole a metal watch he would be executed for theft; if a rich man committed sodomy then his friends in high places were sure to get him released very soon. Wilkes chose to show George III, the government and the aristocracy as being, if not practising sodomites, then at least effeminate supporters of sodomisers. As evidence of this accusation he had only to point the finger at 'the macaroni club', that amorphous group of fops who strutted their stuff around the streets of the capital. Wilkes instead invoked the spirit of England, John Bull, roast beef and respect for women who, he claimed, suffered 'cruel neglect'. Macaronis were demonstrably foreign: if they weren't aping the French they were copying the Italians, and 'everyone knew what the Italians got up to'. Above all, Wilkes managed to place sodomy as a practice enjoyed by aristocrats, not the common man. Soon, in the minds of the British public, being camp and dressing in an effeminate manner with high powdered wigs and using face powder were signs of an immoral lifestyle.

2. The case of HMS *Africaine*

When HMS *Africaine* sailed into Portsmouth harbour in 1815 after four years in the Far East she sparked a series of trials that resulted in four men being hanged, and two men being flogged for 'uncleanness', i.e. deviant sexual behaviour. It was a case that was to rock the Royal Navy because of the evidence of how widespread sodomy had become on this particular ship. It raised important questions about evidence (did an admission of consensual sodomy between two men infer guilt in a case involving a third party?). It also highlighted the perceived link between sodomy and foreigners, particularly Italians (Italy had long been seen by the general populace as being the land of papists, sodomites and catamites). The case predates by exactly one hundred years the comment by Winston Churchill, when he was accused of tampering with naval traditions: 'And what are those traditions? Rum, sodomy and the lash.'

The *Africaine* had been built for the French navy, been captured and recommissioned in the British navy, and had sailed for the East Indies in 1810 under the command of Captain Edward Rodney. She had on board a crew of 350 men. By May 1813 it was already clear that there were 'unclean activities' taking place on board, with suggestions that two midshipmen, Crutchley and Garraway, had been observed committing an offence with the captain's servant boy named John Westerman. Garraway was ordered off the ship; Crutchley was put ashore for six weeks to kick his heels, while Westerman lost his cushy job as a servant and became an ordinary seaman.

At much the same time Emanuel Cross was reported to have been caught performing a sexual act with William Dane. Cross was punished by being placed in leg-irons. The following year led to an inquiry, held in public on the quarter deck, involving two men who were suspected of unclean behaviour. The evidence was inconclusive. In 1815 another incident occurred, in which a crewman called Marbona was accused of trying to bugger a superior officer, who was asleep at the time. The evidence was apparently very limited, and Captain Rodney cast Marbona ashore at Manilla, which was the next port of call, no doubt hoping to sweep everything under the carpet. Rodney's refusal to convict anyone without corroborative evidence was highly commendable, but it seems to have encouraged a feeling on board that 'anything goes'. Within weeks John Westerman's name reappeared in the captain's log, accused of deviant sexual practices. Once more, he was punished (demotion) and banned from the mizzen-top so that he could not corrupt other boys. By October 1815 further lurid tales of immorality and debauchery came to the surface. One of the men, Raphael Seraco, was pressured by Captain Rodney to point the finger at his companions. Seraco did as he was told and implicated another fourteen men involved in a sodomy ring, which Seraco claimed was headed by Raphael Treake. In fact, Seraco and Treake were joint ring-leaders, and as one crewman later testified to the court, 'All the scandalous behaviour in the *Africaine* has been owing to Treake and Seraco.' The fifteen, including Seraco, represented a ring of men willing to engage in not just mutual masturbation but full anal penetrative sex; sometimes in very public situations. The sheer numbers of men implicated in the scandal – forming a nucleus of nearly fifty men – made it impossible for Captain Rodney to do anything positive about the alleged offences: he could hardly string up what amounted to nearly one in five of the whole crew. Instead, he waited until he got back to Portsmouth and handed the whole matter over to the Admiralty to arrange courts martial.

What happened next was not untypical of many trials where to gain a conviction the prosecution proved to be willing to drop charges against one individual, in return for evidence which would enable a successful prosecution to be brought against others. So, evidence was given by one sailor, who was never charged, saying: 'Seraco put the question to me whether I would let him fuck me. I told him I did not much mind. He connected with me forward on the Starboard side. He entered my backside — I did the same with him three times. John Charles the prisoner was the first who mentioned the thing to me or I should never have had such a thought in my head.'

The result was that both Seraco and Charles were sentenced to death, along with young Westerman, mentioned earlier. Treake was also convicted. Both Seraco and Treake were Italian and their crimes were regarded as being in some way typical, and the general feeling was that they had corrupted the others. Sentence of death was carried out on the morning on 1 February 1816. As the ship's log starkly put it: 'a.m. Fresh breezes and cloudy [...] employed getting ready for punishment. At 9 made signal [with] a gun. At 11 executed Seraco, Westerman, Charles, and Treake [for] a breach of the 29th article of war, and punished alongside [John] Parsons [...] with 200 lashes and [Joseph] Hubbard with 170 lashes for a breach of the 2nd article of war as sentenced by a court martial.'

Hubbard received fewer lashes than Parsons because the ship's surgeon intervened to say that death was imminent and the punishment was discontinued. As soon as the punishments had been concluded, the navy ordered an internal investigation into the conduct of Captain Rodney, possibly with a view to charging him with dereliction of duty in allowing the offences to take place. Officers spoke out in his favour, and the inquiry was quickly abandoned. As for the *Africaine*, the decision had already been made to break her up. By the end of 1816 no trace remained of a ship forever associated with one of the most scandalous and sensational cases of the Georgian era.

The four who were executed became part of a shocking statistic: between 1800 and 1835, when the final hanging for sodomy took place, some eighty men paid the ultimate price for this particular crime. The death penalty for the offence of sodomy was reconfirmed under the Offences against the Person Act of 1828: a statute which also made rape, and having carnal knowledge of a girl under the age of ten, a capital offence. In practice the statute was amended several times before being replaced by the Offences against the Person Act of 1861. By then, buggery was punishable by penal servitude for life.

Flogging on board a Royal Navy ship.

Appendix II

The Lady's Dressing Room

The poem entitled *The Lady's Dressing Room* is included here because it throws a light on eighteenth-century attitudes towards individual sexuality, on beauty and on the whole question of physical attractiveness. It was an era when wearing cosmetics became widespread: a reaction against the austere Puritanism of the mid-seventeenth century. Only the poor (and the Quakers, who generally abhorred cosmetics) went make-up free. The poem's publication stirred up an impassioned debate about whether cosmetics were a deception, a trick, a device to give women an upper hand. Beauty, it is often said, is only skin-deep, but if the beauty comes out of a bottle or a jar, men argued that they were seeing not beauty, but beauty disguised.

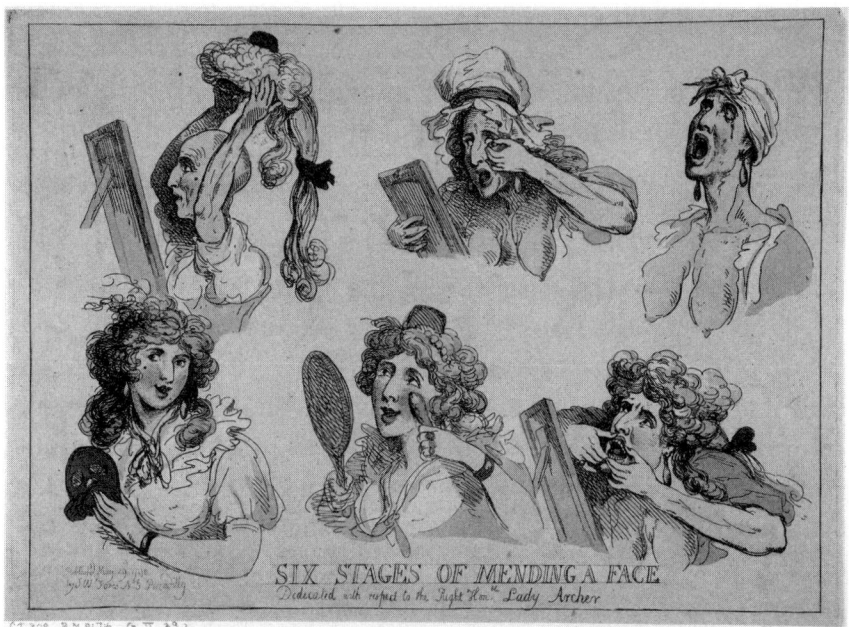

Six Stages of Mending a Face.

Illustrating the poem, the engraving shown on the previous page shows Thomas Rowlandson's savage image of the Six Stages of Mending a Face. It features an old crone at her dressing table, bald, toothless, half-blind and with drooping breasts. She is shown putting on her wig, inserting a glass eye, and fitting false teeth. She dresses herself in fashionable clothing and applies rouge to her cheeks, using a rabbit's foot to softly contour her image, and the end result bears no resemblance to reality. Rowlandson unkindly dedicated the piece to Lady Sarah Archer, famous for her heavy use of cosmetics. Those cosmetics contained large amounts of white lead – known to be poisonous – and Rowlandson was criticizing the vanity of women who sacrificed their own health on the altar of beauty.

Written by Jonathan Swift in 1732, *The Lady's Dressing Room* describes how a man called Strephon steals a peek into his lover Celia's dressing room while she is away. What he sees and smells absolutely disgusts him. It is a poem as much about men's unrealistic expectations as it is about female failings. The deeply satirical blast against women and female beauty aids was seen by some as being blatantly misogynistic. Others saw it as poking fun at the folly of those men who are too blind or too shallow to see that we are all human, and that it was actually written in support of women. Certainly, the travel writer Lady Mary Wortley Montagu did not think so, and published a riposte entitled *The Reasons that Induced Dr. S. to Write a Poem called The Lady's Dressing Room*, in which she suggested that the reason for him writing the poem was sexual frustration. Her poem is about Swift picking up a prostitute but being unable to rise to the occasion:

> The Reverend Lover with surprize,
> Peeps in her Bubbys, and her Eyes,
> And kisses both, and trys — and trys.

Lady Mary hypothesized that Swift blamed the whore for his poor performance, and demanded his money back, but she refused and thereby sparked his diatribe against females in general. In keeping with the scatological content of Swift's poem, and in response to Swift's threat to write in reply, Lady Mary matches Swift's preoccupation with lavatorial matters by ending with the words:

> I'm glad you'll write
> You'll furnish paper when I shite.

Swift was not so much a misogynist as a misanthrope: he loathed all humanity, seeing it as self-absorbed and immoral. Strephon is, in effect, everyman: men are shown as being shallow and unrealistic because they see women as objects. Celia, on the other hand, represents all women: obsessed with beauty and appearances to the point of being vain and devious.

The poem has to be seen in context of the wider debate about whether men were being deceived into marriage by the artifice that went into false wigs, face powder, nipple rouge, tight stays and so on. It is included here as an example of how society was starting to change: how blatant sexuality was, and how naïve men were to fall in love not with the real person but with the outward appearances. One passage from the middle of the poem has been omitted, not for any reason of censorship, but because it does rather go on and on, and then on some more.

> Five hours, (and who can do it less in?)
> By haughty Celia spent in dressing;
> The goddess from her chamber issues,
> Arrayed in lace, brocades and tissues.
> Strephon, who found the room was void,
> And Betty otherwise employed,
> Stole in, and took a strict survey,
> Of all the litter as it lay;
> Whereof, to make the matter clear,
> An inventory follows here.
> And first a dirty smock appeared,
> Beneath the armpits well besmeared.
> Strephon, the rogue, displayed it wide,
> And turned it round on every side.
> On such a point few words are best,
> And Strephon bids us guess the rest,
> But swears how damnably the men lie,
> In calling Celia sweet and cleanly.

Now listen while he next produces
The various combs for various uses,
Filled up with dirt so closely fixt,
No brush could force a way betwixt.
A paste of composition rare,
Sweat, dandruff, powder, lead and hair;
A forehead cloth with oil upon't
To smooth the wrinkles on her front;
Here alum flower to stop the steams,
Exhaled from sour unsavoury streams,
There night-gloves made of Tripsy's hide,
Bequeathed by Tripsy when she died,
With puppy water, beauty's help
Distilled from Tripsy's darling whelp;
Here gallypots and vials placed,
Some filled with washes, some with paste,
Some with pomatum, paints and slops,
And ointments good for scabby chops.
Hard by a filthy basin stands,
Fouled with the scouring of her hands;
The basin takes whatever comes
The scrapings of her teeth and gums,
A nasty compound of all hues,
For here she spits, and here she spews.
But oh! it turned poor Strephon's bowels,
When he beheld and smelled the towels,
Be-gummed, be-mattered, and be-slimed
With dirt, and sweat, and earwax grimed.
No object Strephon's eye escapes,
Here petticoats in frowzy heaps;
Nor be the handkerchiefs forgot
All varnished o'er with snuff and snot.
The stockings why should I expose,
Stained with the marks of stinking toes;
Or greasy coifs and pinners reeking,
Which Celia slept at least a week in?

A pair of tweezers next he found
To pluck her brows in arches round,
Or hairs that sink the forehead low,
Or on her chin like bristles grow.
The virtues we must not let pass,
Of Celia's magnifying glass.
When frightened Strephon cast his eye on't
It showed visage of a giant.
A glass that can to sight disclose,
The smallest worm in Celia's nose,
And faithfully direct her nail
To squeeze it out from head to tail;
For catch it nicely by the head,
It must come out alive or dead.

Thus finishing his grand survey,
Disgusted Strephon stole away
Repeating in his amorous fits,
Oh! Celia, Celia, Celia shits!
But Vengeance, goddess never sleeping
Soon punished Strephon for his peeping;
His foul imagination links
Each Dame he sees with all her stinks:
And, if unsav'ry odours fly,
Conceives a lady standing by:
All women his description fits,
And both ideas jump like wits:
But vicious fancy coupled fast,
And still appearing in contrast.
I pity wretched Strephon blind
To all the charms of female kind;
Should I the queen of love refuse,
Because she rose from stinking ooze?
To him that looks behind the scene,
Satira's but some pocky queen.
When Celia in her glory shows,

If Strephon would but stop his nose
(Who now so impiously blasphemes
Her ointments, daubs, and paints and creams,
Her washes, slops, and every clout,
With which he makes so foul a rout)
He soon would learn to think like me,
And bless his ravished sight to see
Such order from confusion sprung,
Such gaudy tulips raised from dung.

The finishing touch, by James Gillray, showing Lady Sarah Archer applying rouge to her cheeks while sitting at her make-up table.

Bibliography

Annet, Peter, *Social Bliss considered: in Marriage and Divorce, cohabiting unmarried and Public Whoring*, (R. Rose, London, 1749).

Anonymous, *The Tryal of a Cause for Criminal Conversation: Between Theophilus Cibber and William Sloper*, (T. Trott, London 1739).

Anonymous, *Trials for adultery, or, The history of divorces in seven volumes*, (Printed for S. Bladon. London, 1779 and 1780, and available online from Lehigh University Digital Library).

Anonymous, *Aristotle's Masterpiece*, (Third version, London 1712, available as a pdf via Ex-Classics Project at https://www.exclassics.com/arist/arist.pdf)

Anonymous, *A Congratulatory Epistle from a Reformed Rake, to John F------g*, (London 1758).

Anonymous (described as 'An Adept'), *Chrysal: or The Adventures of a Guinea*, (Becket and de Hondt, London, 1768).

Anonymous, *The Machine, Or Love's Preservative. A Poem*, (Printed for T. Reynolds, London, 1744).

Anonymous, *The Benefits and Privileges of Cuckolds* (A. Moore, London 1728).

Anon, *A dialogue between a Married Lady and a Maid*, (London, 1740).

Archenholz, Johann Wilhelm Von, *A Picture of England: Containing a Description of the Laws, Customs and Manners of England* (London, 1789).

Bleackley, Horace, *Ladies Fair and Frail; Sketches of the Demi-Monde in the eighteenth century*, (The Bodley Head, London and New York, 1909).

Boswell, James, *The Journals of James Boswell, 1762–1795*, (Yale University Press, 1994).

Boswell, James, *London Journal 1762–1763*, Ed. F A Pottle, (Yale University Press, 2004).

Browne, John, *The Surgeons Assistant. In which is plainly discovered the True Origin of most Diseases. Treating particularly of the Plague, French Pox, Leprosie, &c.* … (London, 1703).

Buchan, William, *Domestic Medicine, or a Treatise on the Prevention and Cure of Diseases*. (Edinburgh, 1769. Available as a pdf at https://archive.org/details/domesticmedicin00buchgoog/page/n560).

Burg, B.R., *Boys at Sea: Sodomy, Indecency, and Courts Martial in Nelson's Navy*. (Palgrave Macmillan, 2007).

Casanova, Giacamo, *History of My Life*. (Available via Project Gutenberg at http://www.gutenberg.org/ebooks/57691).

Cleland John, *Memoirs of a Woman of Pleasure.* (G. Fenton, London, 1748 (and in its 1749 edition in electronic format at https://www.gutenberg.org/files/25305/25305-h/25305-h.htm).

Corfield, Penelope, *Vauxhall, Sex and Entertainment: London's Pioneering Urban Pleasure Garden.* (History & Social Action Publications 2012).

Cullen, W., *The Edinburgh practice of physic, surgery, and midwifery,* (G. Kearsley, London, 1803).

Culpeper, Nicholas, T*he English Physician* later entitled *The Complete Herbal.* (London 1652. Now available online as *Culpeper's English Physician, and Complete Herbal* at https://archive.org/details/culpeppersenglis00culp/page/n4).

Defoe, Daniel, *Moll Flanders* (W.R Chetwood, London 1722. Available via Project Gutenberg at http://www.gutenberg.org/ebooks/370).

Defoe, Daniel, *A Review of the State of the British Nation.* (Available via Hathi Trust Digital Library at https://catalog.hathitrust.org/Record/000061922).

Defoe, Daniel, *The Fortunes and Misfortunes of the Famous Moll Flanders,* (London 1722).

Defoe, Daniel, *Roxana, the Fortunate Mistress,* (T. Warner, London, 1724).

Farr, Samuel, *Elements of Medical Jurisprudence,* (T. Becket, London,1787).

Fielding, Henry, *The History of Tom Jones, a Foundling,* (London, 1749). Also available via Project Gutenberg at https://www.gutenberg.org/files/6593/6593-h/6593-h.htm).

Grose, Francis, *Dictionary of the Vulgar Tongue,* (S. Hooper, London, 1785, and in its 1811 edition in electronic format via Project Gutenberg at http://www.gutenberg.org/ebooks/5402).

Hunter, John, *Treatise on the Venereal Disease,* (London, 1786).

King, Richard, *The new London Spy; or a Twenty-four hours Ramble through the Bills of Mortality,* (Printed for J. Cooke, Paternoster Road, London, 1771).

La Roche, Sophie von, *1786: Being the Diary of Sophie V. la Roche*, (Jonathan Cape, London, 1933).

Lolme, Jean Louis, *The History of the Flagellants,* (G. Robinson, London, 1783).

Malthus, T.R., *An Essay on the Principle of Population as it Affects the Future Improvement of Society, with Remarks on the Speculations of Mr. Godwin, M. Condorcet, and Other Writers,* (Johnson, London, 1798).

Maubray, John, *The Female Physician,* (James Holland, London 1724).

Meibomius, John Henry, A *Treatise Of the Use of Flogging in Venereal Affairs: Also of the Office of the Loins and Reins,* (E. Curll, London, 1718).

Morgagni, Giovanni Battista, *The Seats and Causes of Diseases Investigated by Anatomy,* (Millar, Cadell, Johnson and Payne, London, 1769).

Moritz, Charles Philip, *Travels in England in 1782,* (Cassell & Co, London, 1886).

Place, Francis, *Illustrations and Proofs of the Principles of Population,* (London, 1822).

Porter, Roy, *Quacks – Fakers and Charlatans in Medicine*, (Tempus Publishing, Stroud, 2001).
Purcell, John, *A Treatise of Vapours, or, Hysterick Fits*, (London, 1702).
Rubenhold, Hallie, *The Covent Garden Ladies*, (Tempus Publishing, Stroud, 2005).
Scull, Andrew, *Hysteria – the Biography*, (Oxford University Press, 2009).
Steele, Elizabeth, *The Memoirs of Sophia Baddeley, late of Drury Lane Theatre*, (London, 1787).
Syson, Lydia, *Doctor of Love – James Graham and his Celestial Bed*, (Alma Books Ltd, 2008).
Szreter, Simon, *Treatment rates for the pox in early modern England: a comparative estimate of the prevalence of syphilis in the city of Chester and its rural vicinity in the 1770s*, (Published online, 11 July 2017 by Cambridge University Press in 'Continuity and Change' https://doi.org/10.1017/S0268416017000212).
Tanner, Anodyne (pseudonym), *The Life Of the late Celebrated Mrs. Elizabeth Wisebourn, Vulgarly call'd Mother Wybourn*, (London, 1721).
Tissot, Samuel Auguste, *L' Onanisme*, (Lausanne, 1760; English edition (*Onanism*) dated 1832 available online https://archive.org/details/57110430R.nlm.nih.gov/page/n41).
Tytler, James, *Ranger's Impartial List of the Ladies of Pleasure in Edinburgh*, (Edinburgh, 1775; and available as a reprint by Paul Harris & Co, 1978).
Ward, Edward, *The Secret History of the London Clubs, or the Citizens Pastime*, (J. Dutton, London, 1709).
Ward, Edward: *The Pleasures of a Single Life: Or, The Miseries of Matrimony. … With the Choice, or the Pleasures of a Country Life*, (London, 1709).
Wilkes, John, *An Essay on Woman*, (London, 1763).
Wilson, Harriette, *The Memoirs of Harriette Wilson, Written By Herself*, (London, 1825; available via Project Gutenberg at http://www.gutenberg.org/ebooks/author/42327).

Online resources
British History online at https://www.british-history.ac.uk/
Journal of the House of Lords, Vol XXXIX (1790) https://books.google.co.uk/books?id=NxtDAAAAcAAJ&pg
The Proceedings of the Old Bailey, 1674–1913: https://www.oldbaileyonline.org/
Rictor Norton's *Homosexuality in Eighteenth-Century England: A Sourcebook*. See http://rictornorton.co.uk/eighteen/
Rictor Norton (ed.), *The First Public Debate about Homosexuality in England: News Reports concerning the Case of Captain Jones, 1772.* http://rictornorton.co.uk/eighteen/jones1.htm
Patrick Spedding's website under the heading Eighteenth Century Erotic Texts online: http://patrickspedding.blogspot.com/2009/07/18ce-texts-online.html

Text Image Accreditation

1. Page vi: 'Fashionable contrasts or – the Duchess's little shoe yielding to the magnitude of the Duke's foot', James Gillray, 1792. Wikimedia. https://commons.wikimedia.org/wiki/File:Fashionable_contrasts_james_gillray.jpg
2. Page x: Sin death and the Devil, by James Gillray, 1792. Library of Congress https://www.loc.gov/resource/cph.3b25518/
3. Page 1: *Cunicularii or The Wise Men of Godliman in Consultation*, William Hogarth. Wikimedia Commons.
4. Page 8: Homunculus in sperm, N. Hartsoeker, Essay de dioptrique, Wellcome Library. (See Wikimedia Commons: https://commons.wikimedia.org/wiki/File:N._Hartsoeker,_Essay_de dioptrique_Wellcome_M0016638.jpg).
5. Page 10: 'The contest between the spirit and the flesh'. Mezzotint from 1773, Wellcome Collection.
6. Page 22: 'The light guinea, or, The blade in the dumps' Carington Bowles 1774. Lewis Walpole Library at Yale University, lwlpr03817
7. Page 23: 'Wouski' by James Gillray. Published by Hannah Humphrey in January 1788. In the public domain.
8. Page 34: 'A peep into Lady W!!!!!y's seraglio' by James Gillray, published by William Humphrey, April 1782. In the public domain.
9. Page 35: Engraving of Sally Salisbury from the *Authentic Memoirs of the Life, Intrigues and Adventures of the Celebrated Sally Salisbury* (1723). Wikimedia.
10. Page 51: 'Tête-à-tête' showing Nancy Parsons and the 3rd Duke of Grafton. 1769, Lewis Walpole Library Collection, lwlpr02768
11. Page 52: Frontispiece, *The School of Venus, Or, The Ladies Delight, Reduced into Rules of Practice*, Michel Millot, translated 1680.
12. Page 61: The Beggar's Benison Test Platter (Photo courtesy of the Museum of the University of St. Andrews).
13. Page 62: Mandrake root. Credit: Science Museum, London. CC BY. Shown courtesy of Wellcome Library.
14. Page 70: Dr Graham pouring out his soul for one shilling. Yale University Lewis Walpole Library, lwlpr35487.
15. Page 71: Casanova blowing up condoms to amuse the ladies, from a print dating from 1872, courtesy of the Library of Congress.
16. Page 80: Condom made from animal gut, tied with ribbon. Photo by Dollymopp.
17. Page 81: Treatment of syphilis by fumigation, 1776, Lalouette. Wellcome Collection
18. Page 93: The Martyrdom of Mercury, John Sintelaer, 1709. Wellcome Images
19. Page 94: Plate 1 of 'The Harlot's Progress' by William Hogarth, CC BY Wellcome Collection.

20. Page 106: 'The Bum-Bailiff outwitted, or, the convenience of fashion'. S.W. Fores, 1786. Lewis Walpole Library lwlpr05966.
21. Page 107: Elizabeth Chudleigh, Duchess of Kingston, brought into court accompanied by her chaplain, physician, apothecary and three maids of honour. 1776 engraving by J.H. Mortimer, shown courtesy of the Wellcome Collection. CC BY
22. Page 115: Retail traders not subject to shop tax, 1787. Library of Congress.
23. Page 116: The Jelly House Maccaroni, printed for Carington Bowles in 1772, © The Trustees of the British Museum. CC BY-NC-SA 4.0
24. Page 125: 'An evening's invitation; with a wink from the Bagnio', printed for Carington Bowles, 1773. Library of Congress. In the public domain.
25. Page 126: Captain Edward Rigby, mezzotint print by John Smith, Scottish National Portrait Gallery, Print Room. In the public domain.
26. Page 139: 'The Woman Haters Lamentation' per Wikimedia Commons. In the public domain.
27. Page 140: 'The Discovery', by Thomas Rowlandson, drawn in 1799. In the public domain.
28. Page 152: Chevalier d'Eon, extract from an engraving. In the public domain, shown courtesy of the Lyons Bibliotheque Municipale.
29. Page 153: 'A Music Maker tuning his instrument', by Thomas Rowlandson. In the public domain.
30. Page 163: 'Cunnyseurs', by Thomas Rowlandson. In the public domain.
31. Page 165: 'Sex around a country cottage' – Thomas Rowlandson. In the public domain, per Wikimedia Commons.
32. Page 168: 'Goodbye', drawn by Thomas Rowlandson. In the public domain, per Wikimedia Commons.
33. Page 169: 'Captain Jones as the Firework Macaroni', shown courtesy of the Rijksmuseum.
34. Page 176: Flogging on board a naval ship, after George Cruikshank's *The Point of Honour*. In the public domain.
35. Page 177: 'Six Stages of Mending a Face', by Thomas Rowlandson, for S.W. Fores, 1792. Metropolitan Museum.
36. Page 182: 'The finishing touch', by James Gillray. Shown courtesy of the Lewis Walpole Library, lwlpr07229.

Accreditation for Plates
Plate 1a: 'Harris's list; or, Cupid's London directory', 1794, by Richard Newton. (Courtesy of the Library of Congress).
Plate 1b: 'Dressing for a Masquerade', by Thomas Rowlandson. (Courtesy of the Metropolitan Museum).
Plate 2a: 'Mademoiselle de Beaumont or, The Chevalier D'Eon'. (Library of Congress).
Plate 2b: The Whore's last shift', by James Gillray, 1779. (Library of Congress).

188 Sex and Sexuality in Georgian Britain

Plate 3a: 'The Macaroni – a real character at the late masquerade'. Mezzotint by Philip Dawe, 1773. (Wikimedia Commons).
Plate 3b: A dildo: dictionary definition. Taken from Blackguardiana: Or, A Dictionary of Rogues by James Caulfield, c.1793.
Plate 4a: 'Cupid as a link boy', by Reynolds. (Courtesy of The Metropolitan Museum).
Plate 4b: 'Mercury and his advocates defeated', by Thomas Rowlandson, 1789. (Wellcome Collection. Gallery Library reference: ICV No 11173).
Plate 5a: 'A Morning Frolic – or the Transmutation of the Sexes', by John Collet, 1782. (Yale University Center for British Art, Paul Mellon collection).
Plate 5b: Plate V from 'Marriage a la Mode', by William Hogarth. (Metropolitan Museum of Art).
Plate 6a: 'The Cully Flaug'd'. (Courtesy of the Rijksmuseum).
Plate 6b: 'A fool and his money's soon parted'. Published by R. Sayer, 1790. (Lewis Walpole Library). lwlpr06914.
Plate 7a: 'A St Giles Beauty'. Printed by Carington Bowles, 1784. (Lewis Walpole Library). lwlpr05402.
Plate 7b: 'A St James Beauty'. Published by Carington Bowles, 1784.
Plate 8a: Dr Rock selling his wares, 1743. (Wellcome Collection CC BY).
Plate 8b: Plate 5 of William Hogarth's *A Harlot's Progress*.

Index

Abington, Frances 47, 161
Archenholz, Johann W. D. 13–4, 120, 137–8, 141, 147, 183
Abortifacients 76–7
Anal sex 73, 75, 136
Annet, Peter 154–5, 182
Aphrodisiacs **61–9**, 119
Armistead, Elizabeth 19, 29, 48
Austen, Jane 158–9

Baddeley, Sophia **37**, 185
Bagnigge Wells 12, 122
Bagnios 16, 19, 20, 42, 82, **116–21**, 125, 147
Beggar's Benison 61
Berkley, Theresa 145–7
Bestiality **112**, 128
Bigamy **106–11**, 137
Bonny, Anne 143
Boswell, James 85–8, 117, 166, 183
Breastfeeding 76
Brothels 15–8, 27–30, 48, 54–5, 82, 102, 104, **106–24**, 131–2, 136, 142, 145, 155, 161, 166
Buchan, William 90–1, 183
Burney, Fanny 158–9

Calvert, Frederick 104
Casanova 20, 40–1, 65, 71, 73, 78, 87–8, 118, 120, 183
Charteris, Francis 36, 94, 101–4, 123
Cholmondeley, Lord 44, 48, 124, 150
Chudleigh, Elizabeth **107–10**, 136, 167
Clap, Margaret 114, 134–5

Cleland, John 8, 38, 55, 75, 82, 99, 141, 145, 154, 157–8, 184
Condoms 71, 76, 79–80, 83, 86, 88–9, 117
Courtenay, William 128, 167
Covent Garden:17, 19, 42, 47, 60, 92, 118–9
Criminal Conversation 9, 27, 32, 156, 182
Cross dressing 125, 131, **147–8**, 151
Cruikshank, George 29
Cruikshank, Isaac 29
Culpeper, Nicholas 65, 77, 184

d'Eon, Chevalier 151–2
Defoe, Daniel 17, 82, 132, 153, 157–8, 167. 184
Dickens, Charles 139
Dildos **51–61**, 149, 150

Elliott, Grace Dalrymple **44**, 150

Farr, Samuel 95, 184
Fielding, Henry 19, 55, 60, 82, 148–9, 184
Fielding, John 19, 136
Fisher, Kitty **40–2**
Flagellation **141–7**, 157
Foote, Samuel 137–8
Fox, Charles James 19, 46, 48–9
Frotting 73

Galen (Claudius Galenus) 3, 58–9, 62, 66
George I 2, **24–5**, 102, 168

George II **25–6**, 36, 103
George III 9, 24, **27**, 64, 67, 69, 72, 111, 136, 143, 173
George IV (formerly Prince of Wales) 7, 9, **28–30**, 45, 48, 50, 150, 161
Gillray, James 7, 23, 29, 118, 160–1, 182
Green sickness 5
Graham, James 67–70
Grose, Francis 5, 20, 56, 74, 184

Harrington, Lady Caroline 145
Harris's List 17, 38, 42, 47, 74–5, 118, 121
Hayes, Charlotte 122–3, 161
Hellfire Club 38, 61, 162
Hogarth, William 1, 67, 82, 92, 94, 103, 121, 123, 159–60
Hunter, John 63–4, 184
Hunter, William 4
Hysteria 6–7, 57–9, 185

Incest 25, 101, 158
Infanticide 77

Jones, Captain Robert 136, **168–72**

King, Molly 119

Ladies of Llangollen 142–3
La Roche, Sophie von 13, 67, 184
Link boys 127

Macaronis 75, 119, 131, 136, 169, 173
Mahon, Gertrude **43–4**, 150
Masquerades 9, 88, 125, 131, 149–51
Masturbation 57–61, 73, 83
Maubray, John 2, 6–8, 184
Mercury 16, 81, 89–91, 93
Molly house 134–5, 139
Morning Post 43, 46, 129
Murray, Fanny **37**, 61, 162

Needham, Elizabeth 123
New Female Coterie 33, 145

O'Brien, Nelly **42–3**
Old Bailey 14, 96–8, 103, 108, 114, 134, 139, 168
Oral sex 73–5

Parsons, Nancy 19, 39, 51
Pitt, William 7, 129
Pridden, Sarah – see Salisbury, Sally

Ranelagh Gardens 12, 16, 117, 122, 150–1
Rape 17, 78, **93–105**, 108, 111, 157, 166, 176
Read, Mary 143–4
Reynolds, Sir Joshua 40, 42, 47, 128, 161
Richardson, Samuel 55, 153
Rigby, Edward 126, 132
Robinson, Mary 29, **45–8**, 152, 161
Rowlandson, Thomas 61, 125, 140, 160–1, 163, 165, 178
Rock, Richard 92

Salisbury, Sally **35–6**, 123
Sapphism 125, 141–2
Sodomy 66, 112, 114, 125, 127, 130–2, 134–8, 168, 172–6
Spencer, Georgiana (Duchess of Devonshire) 31, 69
Swainson, Isaac 93
Swift, Jonathan 101, 104, 178–9

Tarleton, Banastre 46–7
Temple of Hymen & Health 67–9
Tissot, Samuel Auguste 57–8, 185
Toft, Mary 1–3
Town & Country Magazine 20, 39, 145

Vauxhall Gardens 12, 16, 117, 122, 150–1, 184

Velno's Vegetable Syrup 93
Venereal Disease vii, 10, 14, 33–4, 57, 64, 70, 79–87, 91–3, 96, 101
Virginity **51–7**, 73, 97, 154

Wallace, William 91
Walpole, Horace 19, 25–6, 39, 103–4, 130–1, 141, 151, 164

Wilkes, John xiii, 162–4, 173, 185
William IV **30**, 49, 161, 168
Wilson, Harriette **49–50**, 155, 185
Wollstonecraft, Mary ix, 152
Worsley, Lady Seymour 32, 34

Zoffany, Johan 88